H· ·l · 1 ᴰ d

to]   e

D0916330

Acknowledgements

Keith Amburgey

Lane Boldman

Stuart Butler

Dave Cooper

Mary Carol Cooper

Donna DePenning

Oscar Geralds, Jr.

Jorge Hershel

Liz Kauffman

Wally Mastropaolo

Mary Nell McGary

Darren Payne

Martha Payne

Bill Pierskalla

Terese Pierskalla

Jessie Pierskalla

Joey Shadowen

Amy Stawicki

Dave Stawicki

Lucas Stone

Jay Taylor

Kate Taylor

Jeannine Walker

Janet Worne

Eve Yost

Greg Zahradnik

The members of the
Bluegrass Group Sierra Club
respectfully and lovingly
dedicate this book to

Mr. Oscar Geralds, Jr.

whose dedication to protect the
Red River Gorge
made this book possible.

© 2000 Harmony House Publishers Louisville
P.O. Box 90
Prospect, Kentucky 40059
502-228-2010

Library of Congress Number 99-75583
International Standard Book Index Number 1-56469-066-0

Printed in Canada

*Front Cover: A four-hour time exposure of Sky Bridge at night
reveals trails of stars in the sky. Photo by Janet Worne*

About the Sierra Club

The Sierra Club motto is "to explore, enjoy, and protect the wild places of the earth; to practice and promote the responsible use of the earth's ecosystems and resources; to educate and enlist humanity to protect and restore the quality of the natural and human environment; and to use all lawful means to carry out these objectives."

The Sierra Club was founded in 1892 by John Muir, a visionary, intellectual and outdoorsman. Long before our present "conservation movement," he foresaw the need to protect our wilderness heritage.

Since its founding, the Sierra Club has grown into an international organizationof almost 580,000 members. Today, the Sierra Club continues its dedication to the two important goals established by John Muir: enjoying our environment through outing programs and conserving and protecting our environment through legislative and political activities.

The Sierra Club is governed by a main office in San Francisco, and regional branches of Chapters and Groups throughout the United States. To join, write to Sierra Club, 85 Second Street, 2nd Floor, San Francisco, CA 94105 or contact our national website at www.sierraclub.org.

Contents

This book is the compilation, of the efforts of many people. We come from different places, with very different backgrounds, but we all share one deeply rooted passion, a love of the wilderness of the Red River Gorge.

We are members of the Bluegrass Group of the Sierra Club, the oldest, organized conservation group in the country. In our words, lifestyles and efforts we promote the exploration, preservation and stewardship of the the wilderness that we find so important to our well being as citizens and persons.

When the opportunity to write this book was first brought to us, we debated its necessity and how it would impact the "Gorge", which we work hard to protect. It was our decision and is our hope, that by providing a comprehensive guide to the trails and

natural beauty of this area, that many more people will grow to care for it and help us to preserve this unique place which we have and continue to explore and maintain.

The Red River Gorge and Natural Bridge State Park are becoming increasingly impacted by an increase in user population, accessibility and growing publicity. When considering how these things are affecting the beauty of these places, we decided to write this book to provide useful, safe and considerate information to the public.

We ask and encourage you to follow the guidelines and regulations of the Forestry Service and Parks Department, and for ourselves we ask one simple thing... *take only photographs and leave only footprints.*

For hundreds of thousands of years the river called "The Red" flowed peacefully and unencumbered through the majestic Gorge, below impressive cliff lines, passing through ancient forests, along sand bars, around huge boulders, often forming quiet pools, then through violent rapids. During periods when the rain did not fall, the river would diminish, slowly and the remaining pools offered refuge to many creatures. When the rains would come, the river awakened showing its great strength, rushing powerfully, reaching out to the lowlands adjoining the normal river bed to reclaim the nearby areas which belonged to the river.

The Red River
A Flow of Time

In due time, humans came in to the area—first to hunt and to gather, later raising primitive crops; some lingering for longer terms. Hunting parties traveling from both the north and south came to harvest the abundant wildlife which lived a sheltered life in the Gorge.

More recent times brought the "explorer" from areas such as Virginia and North Carolina with names such as "D. Boon."

Settlements began to form on the lower Red River downstream from the mostly uninhabitable Gorge area. Resources were extracted such as iron, saltpetre, oil and timber. The river became an avenue to transport the enormous logs harvested from the hillsides of the Gorge. Small, but temporary dams would be constructed to hold the floating timber until it was released for the trip to the downstream mills. The river may also have been used to transport a 'product' produced by transforming the local grain crop into a more transportable liquid.

During all of this time the Red River continued to flow freely. As the timber on the Gorge hillsides replenished itself, the grandeur of the Red River Gorge persisted.

In the early part of this century, a few citizens residing in a small town downstream from the Gorge contacted the United States Corps of Engineers. On occasion, the Red River would reclaim portions of the land which would impact upon this community, and the residents sought help in the construction of a flood wall. After many years of deliberation, the Corps answered, advising the citizens that they did not need a relatively inexpensive and efficient flood wall, but actually needed a massive dam upsteam to "control" the beautiful Red River. The Corps designed a dam to be constructed on the Red near Indian Creek. This would have completely flooded the most scenic and pristine portion of the Gorge. Thus began the long, bitter and hurtful controversy of the proposed "Red River Dam."

The Gorge was not widely visited, nor was it familiar to many people. There were those who saw land development possibilities, added water resources, power boat recreational potential and other economic windfalls. They saw the pristine wilderness that was invaluable in its undeveloped state. A few members of the newly formed Cumberland Chapter of the Sierra Club took issue with this proposal and launched a major campaign to prevent what they saw as an impending major tragedy.

Opponents of the proposed dam began a major public education campaign. Supreme Court Justice William O. Douglas led a hike in the Gorge that brought national attention to the issue. Scientific studies were conducted, many testified at Congressional hearings, wrote letters, and tried to inform the public. Ultimately the Corps withdrew this proposal for "further study." However, a few years later they came forward with another proposal for a new dam to be constructed near Bowen. While this would have spared a small portion of the upper Gorge from flooding, it now would take the homes and farms of people who had occupied the area for generations. At least one farm family traced their family ownership back to a land patent signed by Patrick Henry.

Once again, those who saw the value of the Red River Gorge as a natural treasure rose up. A large coalition was formed by the Sierra Club, other conservation organizations, local citizens, scientists, historians, students and many others. A campaign to inform the public now extended nationwide. Articles appeared in *Audubon, Time, Southern Living* and other national magazines. Tens of thousands of bumper stickers admonished all to "Stop the Dam—Save the Red River Gorge," and newspapers were inundated with letters. Congressional committees received the message through testimony and then a lawsuit was filed in Federal District Court, which resulted in a temporary injunction. The lawsuit made possible the discovery of many documents and much information concerning the proposal. Experts in many fields; (biology, zoology, economics, law) donated their services freely. Large protests were staged, including an impressive march to the State Capitol.

Finally, the Govenor advised the Corps that the State was no longer interested in the proposed dam on the Red River and the plan was "put on the shelf." The national outcry had, for the time being, saved the Red River Gorge from flooding, but the publicity had greatly increased the visitation, creating the fear that the area would be "loved to death." While some areas are now extremely popular at times, the trails and back country still remain pristine and furnish the feeling of wilderness and solitude.

The ensuing years have called upon the viligance of those who care for the Gorge. Threats continue from nearby timbering, upriver stripmining, oil extraction and other intrusions. After many years and much effort by dedicated individuals, in 1994 a significant portion of the Red River was designated for protection under the Federal Wild and Scenic River program.

At the present time the Red River still flows unencumbered through the majestic Gorge. It is our hope and prayers that this will never end.

A view of Half Moon Rock from Chimney Top

The Daniel Boone National Forest

The Daniel Boone National Forest was named to honor the well-known wilderness explorer who brought early settlers to Kentucky. Located in the mountains of eastern Kentucky, the Forest is divided into seven ranger districts encompassing about 682,000 acres in portions of 21 counties.

The Forest lies within the Northern Cumberland Plateau region. This area is a transition zone between the northern forest types (dominated by beech, sugar maple, white pine and hemlock) and southern forest types (dominated by several kinds of oaks and hickories). The mixed mesophytic forest community, known for its rich diversity of plant species, also flourishes here.

The terrain is generally rugged, with steep slopes and narrow valleys, towered by extensive rock & limestone cliffs. This landscape provides habitat for threatened and endangered species, including the red-cockaded woodpecker, Indiana bat, Virginia big-eared bat, and White-haired Goldenrod. Over 100 species of birds, 46 species of mammals, and 67 types of reptiles and amphibians thrive in the forest.

Recreation

The Daniel Boone National Forest lies within a six-hour drive for over 23 million people. The Forest can be reached via I-64 and I-75, the Bert T. Combs Mountain Parkway and other major roads.

There are many opportunities for visitors to enjoy its streams, lakes and wooded areas. Popular activities include hiking, camping, picnicking, hunting, fishing, boating, swimming, horseback riding, bicycling, rock climbing, spelunking, bird watching, photography, nature study, and more.

The Daniel Boone National Forest has the largest trail system in Kentucky, with nearly 500 miles of trails, including two National Recreation Trails. Some of the trails are designed for multiple-users, while others are reserved for foot travel only.

There are two designated wildernesses in the Forest that encompass a total of 18,000 acres. Two major lakes - Cave Run Lake, Laurel Lake - and part of a third one are managed by the Forest Service. There are three white water rivers in the Forest - the Red, Rockcastle and Cumberland Rivers. The majority of streams managed for trout fishing are located in the Forest. The large concentration of caves in the Forest represent what may be the greatest unexplored subterranean resource in the eastern United States.

There are 28 campgrounds and 22 picnic areas in the Forest. A fee is charged at group picnic areas and many of the campgrounds, based on the facilities provided at those sites. Family picnic areas and boat ramps may be used free of charge. Most of the developed recreation areas in the Forest are open from the middle of April to the first of November. Recreation use is highest from Memorial Day to Labor Day, with the spring wildflower season and the fall leaf-color season being especially popular.

Bluegrass Group Members on the Sheltowee

Sheltowee Trace National Recreation Trail

The "Sheltowee" (shell - toe' - wee) is a 254 mile long multiple-use trail that extends the full length of the Daniel Boone National Forest. Sheltowee (meaning "Big Turtle") was the name given to Daniel Boone when he was adopted into the Shawnee tribe as the son of the great war chief, Blackfish.

The Sheltowee Trace meanders through the Red River Gorge along high, narrow ridges and rim rock cliffs, then dropping into deep gorges to follow the paths of small streams in the area. A great variety of trees, wildflowers, birds and animals may be found in the diverse habitat along the trail.

The Sheltowee Trace Trail was designated as the 100th trail in the National Trail System. It is open to many uses, including back-

packing, camping, hiking and hunting. Signs are posted to indicate the trail sections that are open to foot travel only.

Red River Gorge Geological Area

The Red River Gorge Geological Area is a unique and scenic natural area that is home to over 100 natural sandstone arches. Carved by wind and water over time, the Red River Gorge is characterized by steep sandstone cliffs, overhanging rock ledges, and narrow, boulder-strewn valleys. The complex topography provides habitat for a rich diversity of plants and animals, including many rare species.

The 26,000 acre Geological Area has been designated a National Natural Landmark. It is managed for year-round public use and enjoyment, as well as protection of its watersheds, wildlife, unique geologic features and primitive character.

Clifty Wilderness

The Clifty Wilderness is a rugged, undeveloped area within the Red River Gorge, encompassing most of the northern and eastern region. This 13,000 acre woodlands features arches, rock shelters and towering cliffs encircling steep, forested slopes and narrow stream valleys. The rugged topography offers physical challenges as well as opportunities for quiet and solitude. This region of the Gorge contains about 20 miles of trails including parts of the Sheltowee Trace, Swift Camp Creek Trail, Wildcat Trail, as well as unnamed trails which may be developed in the near future. Wilderness areas are roadless and offer trails that tend to be more rugged and less developed. Highway #715 forms the dividing boundry between the Gorge and Clifty Wilderness, where trailheads can be accessed.

Types of Woodlands

The Red River Gorge follows the Pottsville escarpment on the eastern edge of the Cumberland Plateau.

Upland vegetation consisting of dry pine and oak woods occur on the higher areas, while mixed mesophytic forest communities predominate at lower elevations. The mixed mesophytic community is the most complex and oldest forest association in eastern North America. These forests are characterized by moist, well drained soils and a thick layer of humus. Instead of a few dominant species, dominance is shared by 20 or 25 species, especially tulip poplar, sugar maple, beech, basswood, yellow buckeye, red oak, white oak, red maple, hemlock, black walnut, black cherry, shagbark hickory, white pine, and white ash.

The mesophytic forest usually consists of four strata: upper canopy which consists of dominant species; lower canopy;, shrub layer; and the ground layer consisting of herbs, ferns, and mosses.

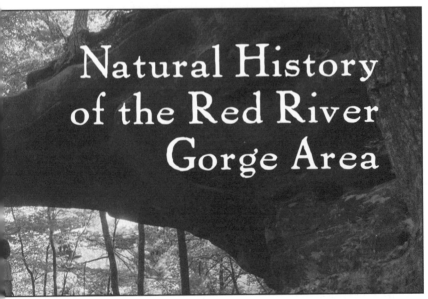

Princess Arch

Birds

The Red River Gorge area is a wonderful place for bird watchers all year round. There are more than 100 species of birds here. A study was done in 1995-96 which showed that the abundance and density of the avian population in this area has not decreased in the past 15 years because the area has not been fragmented or urbanized like much of Kentucky.

In April and May, one is likely to see plenty of migrating birds going to their breeding areas. In September through October, they pass through again to winter in the south. Summer residents are vocal during breeding season and are usually easier to hear, see, and identify. Most of the time, the birds of the forest are much easier to identify by their song due to the lack of visibility. A checklist of the more common birds that you may come across from May to September can be found in the back of this book.

There are 18 species of warblers who are summer residents on the Cumberland Plateau. Several of them are quite abundant and are very vocal during breeding season. It is always fun to learn their songs to make identification easier.

Flora and Fauna

The geology of the Red River Gorge contributes to the interesting group of plants and animals found in the area. The high sandstone cliffs provide unique habitats for many species. Green salamanders tuck into shady moist crevices in the rock face and can often be seen with a carefully aimed flashlight. Some species of plants such as Lucy Braun's white snakeroot and white-haired goldenrod have adapted to live in the sandy and often dry soils below cliffs. White-haired goldenrod is a threatened species that can be found nowhere else in the world. Even though it can thrive in a dry environment, it is extremely sensitive to foot traffic. In many places, hikers have trampled and killed the plants and compacted the soil so they cannot regrow.

Bats also use the cliff line, but are much more mobile, thus using more of the cliff line. At night, several species of bats use the cliff line as feeding routes. The gap between the sides of the cliff and the adjacent trees is often much easier to fly through than the clutter of the nearby forest. While sleeping during the day, the eastern small-footed bat wedges itself into small cracks in the cliff face—often in crevices no higher than 3/4 of an inch. In contrast, Virginia big-eared bats (an endangered species) and Rafinesque's big-eared bats (a sensitive species) find large dark cracks and rock shelters in which to roost. These areas may also be used by large groups of females in the spring and summer to raise their young. The shelters selected maintain a special temperature which helps the newborn bats develop quickly. These maternity roosts are special and sensitive areas. Disturbing them can cause the mothers to abandon the roost, often leaving their babies behind. They then must select a new site that may not be as suitable for raising their young. If you think you see bats, talk quietly and leave quickly. Report the location of these special animals to Forest Service staff as soon as you can.

The presence of cliff lines in the Red River Gorge also produces a phenomenon known as 'cold air drainage'. Sunlight is prevented from reaching the slopes of narrow drains and ravines for much of the day, and as the cold air falls, it is pulled into the low-lying areas. This is in contrast to what happens on many mountains, where the coldest areas are on top. Consequently, many species of plants were able to survive here as the glaciers retreated northward. These species are known as 'northern relics' because their closest relatives are located in the colder climes of the northern part of the country. Many species that you would expect to find on the tops of tall mountains can be found in the ravines of the Red River Gorge. These include red-berried elderberry, mountain maple, shining ladies' tresses, and Canada yew.

Tucked into the narrow ravines are beautiful creeks, all flowing to the Red River. The Red River was designated a National Wild and Scenic River in 1995 because of its water quality and lack of development. Living in the waters are a number of native sport fishes such as muskellunge, bluegill, and large and smallmouth bass. Trout are also present in the area as the result of stocking with the Kentucky Department of Fish and Wildlife Resources and the U. S. D. A. Forest Service. Portions of the Red River, Indian Creek, and the Middle Fork of the Red River are stocked yearly to sustain a put-and-take fishery. But the Red and its tributaries host more than just sport fish. Smaller fish such as darters and daces are colorful and important additions. These species serve as food sources for the larger fish and also help keep the streams clean. Some species such as the

Eastern sand darter and the redside dace are sensitive species that remind us of the importance of keeping our waterways free of silt and pollution.

The quality of the Red River is especially important to the diverse numbers of mussels that can be found here. Twenty-three species are known to inhabit the Red River. Many include sensitive species with such colorful names as salamander mussel, elktoe, and the round hickory nut whose populations are among the best in the state. Other, more common species including kidneyshell, spike, threeridge and pistolgrip can be found throughout the Red River drainage.

In the southern and northeastern sections of the area, the sandstone cliff lines are underlain by a layer of limestone. Because limestone is easily dissolved in water, sinks and caves of various sizes have been formed. These karst features are important and fragile resources. Caves are used by many species of bats for winter hibernation sites. Like rock shelters, not all sites are suitable. The temperature and air flow must be just right in order for the bats to be able to make it through the winter. Several of the caves in the area are gated because they support large populations of the endangered Indiana and Virginia big-eared bats. Disturbance from visitors can waken the bats and cause them to use significant amounts of their stored fat. It is estimated that each time a bat wakes up, it uses between 7 and 30 days worth of stored energy.

Common game species such as white-tailed deer, fox squirrel, turkey, grouse and quail are prevalent. Although some of the area is closed to hunting, seeing these animals can still give an outdoors person a thrill. Bobcat and coyote are present, though their secretive nature makes a sighting rare. Black bear have even been seen in the eastern portion of the area. Black bear were once common in Kentucky and now, thanks to successful management in surrounding states, this species is also calling Kentucky home. Black bear are private animals that primarily eat grasses, fruits and berries, insects and carrion.

Few people think of amphibians and reptiles when they think about the diversity of wildlife. The forests of the area support a large range of both groups of animals. Amphibians prefer wet or moist places. Salamanders can be found under logs at the edge of ponds, in the many creeks running through the area and at fresh springs. Many of these species are showy and easily identified. Common species include tiger, marbled, spotted and spring salamanders. Look along the edges of still water or listen on a warm spring or summer night for frogs. It is often easy to find wood frogs, American toads, Copeís gray treefrogs, green frogs, pickerel frogs and spring peepers.

As for reptiles, keep your eyes out for turtles such as the common snapping turtle, eastern box turtle, and the red-eared slider. Lizards include several species of skinks and the northern fence lizard. There are only two species of venomous snakes here, the northern copperhead and the timber rattlesnake (which is on a decline). Neither of these snakes are deadly if a bite is treated within a reasonable time. Some other snakes that you may encounter are the worm snake, black racer, black rat snake, and eastern garter snake. Again, keep in mind, there are only two venomous snakes in the Red River Gorge and they don't want to see you anymore than you want to see them!

Wildflowers

Several of the trails in this book are noted for outstanding spring wildflowers. In the gorge area, Rock Bridge, Whittleton Branch and Whittleton Arch, Swift Camp Creek and Wildcat Trails are outstanding in the spring as are Rock Garden Trail and the

Original Trail at Natural Bridge State Resort Park. There is also part of a non-marked trail from the Sheltowee parking lot off of KY highway 715 to the swinging bridge over the Red River which harbors a profusion of wildflowers in April and May. There you can see almost any spring wildflower that you want to see.

Red River Gorge is home to a host of gorgeous spring wildflowers, and there are beautiful, blooming plants here all throughout the growing season. The mountain laurel blooms in mid to late May and the rhododendron begins blooming in late June through early July. In May and June on a trip through the gorge, large white blossoms can be seen at the tops of fairly tall, skinny trees. These are blooms of our 4 native magnolias: umbrella, big leaf, cucumber, and tulip poplar (our state tree). In fall, asters, joe-pye weed, sunflowers, iron weed, and goldenrod add splendid flashes of color to the forests of Red River Gorge. (checklist at end of book.)

The Low Impact Visitor

The Red River Gorge is a delicate, fragile environment used by thousands of visitors each year. The combined impact of this use is tremendous, causing many people to believe that we are "loving the Gorge to death." Every use is a serious environmental impact and we ask that all visitors follow simple guidelines to minimize their impact on the area. By following these low-impact (Leave No Trace!) guidelines, you not only help protect the forest, but also lessen the sights and sounds of your trip so others can enjoy the woods at the same time.

Hiking

Hike in single file and stay on marked trails avoiding short-cuts, such as cutting corners on switchbacks or trying to go around a muddy spot in the middle of the trail. Cutting corners on switchbacks creates new scars on hillsides, causes erosion of the hillside and breaks down the trail. As hikers avoid muddy areas, the trail gets continuously wider and begins to look like a road rather than a trail.

Leave the trees, bushes, flowers, rocks, archaeological sites, etc. as you see them so others can enjoy them. This also includes trail signs and markers. Disturbing trail signs and markers may cause hikers to get lost. Take only pictures.

Try to keep the size of your group small. A smaller group has less impact on the environment.

If you do any off-trail hiking, spread out and don't walk single file. Hiking off-trail in single file will only create new trails.

Remember, you are probably not the only one in the woods, so try not to make excessively loud noises which may disturb other hikers, and leave the radios and boom-boxes at home.

Camping

Make your camp at least 300 ft. from the trail and 200 ft. from all water sources, and also be aware of game paths so you don't block an animal's usual path to food, water or general travel. If possible, arrange your camp so it's not visible from the trail.

Buy equipment in natural colors (such as green, gray or brown) that blend in with the woods.

The best place to camp is at designated campsites or areas that are already well-established so impact is concentrated in these already disturbed places. In little used areas, try to move your camp to a new location every night. It takes about two weeks for a site to recover from one night's camping and an entire season to recover from two nights at the same site.

If there is more than one tent in your group, spread tents over a large area and use a common kitchen and campfire area to minimize impact.

Pack out EVERYTHING you carried in, including all garbage and food. Human food is not healthy for animals and they will find it even if buried. Once animals learn campers/backpackers are a source of food they will become a nuisance and may have to be relocated or destroyed.

Restore or naturalize your campsite before you leave by fluffing-up or scattering the leaves under your tent and around the campsite, replacing rocks or twigs you moved, etc. There should be no obvious signs that the area was a campsite.

Campfires

Check fire regulations before you head into the woods to make sure campfires are allowed in the area.

If your campsite is in a well-established area and a fire ring is present, use the existing fire ring. DO NOT create a new one!! If your campsite does not have an existing fire ring, scrape off all the leaves, pine needles and mineral soil (top soil) and put aside before building your campfire. Do not line the ring with rocks, since you have to disturb rocks and anything living under them, and the fire will leave black marks on the rocks.

Keep your fire small, burning wood no bigger around than your arm. Use only down and dead wood and gather your wood from a wide-ranging area away from your campsite (but be aware of the vegetation you are trampling to gather wood). Make sure all the wood burns completely to ash. Partially burned logs and charcoal are hard to hide and take a very long time to break down.

Burn only wood in your campfire. DO NOT burn garbage or leftover food, animals can smell leftover residues from burned food and will dig up the campsite looking for it. PACK IT OUT.

Make sure your fire is completely out before leaving the campsite, pouring water on the coals, stirring them around until they are cold to the touch. The remaining ash should be carried away from the campsite and scattered widely, as should any remaining stacks of wood you did not burn. Replace the top soil and scatter the area with leaves.

It's also helpful to dismantle abandoned fire rings you might encounter while out on the trail.

Sanitation

Do not wash your dishes or yourself in water sources. Even using biodegradable soap can upset the balance of the water and animals living in the water. Carry water to a spot 200 yards from the source to do your washing and if you absolutely have to use soap, make sure it is biodegradable.

Human waste should be buried in "cat holes" - holes dug about 6-8" deep and 200 yards from any water sources or camp. Make sure any toilet paper used is also either buried in the cat hole or packed out. Some people advocate burning the tissue, but be aware of fire regulations in effect before you do this. If you choose to bury your toilet paper, it's best to choose paper with no dyes or perfumes. Most people hike, camp or backpack to enjoy nature and a "wilderness experience" and may also be seeking an escape from crowds, phone, traffic and other daily pressures of urban life. Please respect the rights of others using the trails and practice low-impact hiking and camping on your visit to the Red River Gorge so everyone will enjoy their visit.

For more information on the 'Leave No Trace!' ethic, call 1-800-332-4100.

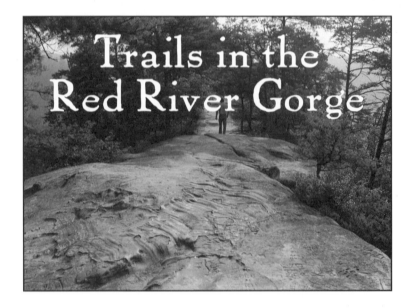

Trails in the Red River Gorge

F ollowing are descriptions of the trails you will find in The Red River Gorge Geological Area, Clifty Wilderness and Natural Bridge State Park. These trails were scouted by Sierra Club volunteers from fall of 1997 to spring of 1998, and the descriptions are a result of their observations and experiences.

In addition, here is some general information regarding these trails.

Maps

The USDA-Forest Service prints a map which is a composite topographical map encompassing Red River Gorge and Clifty Wilderness. It is based on the USGS quads of Slade, KY and Pomeroyton, KY. The composite map can be purchased from the Forest Service or several Kentucky outfitters. USGS quads can be purchased at some outfitters or through map houses that specialize in topos, as well as from the Forest Service.

Natural Bridge State Park prints a small brochure that you

can get for free at Hemlock Lodge. This map is more "artistic" than topographic, but the trails here are well marked and easy to follow.

Trailheads

All descriptions of trailheads are based on starting at the Junior Williamson Rest Area at the junction of KY 15 and The Bert T. Combs Mountain Parkway. This junction is 33 miles east of Winchester, KY where the Mountain Parkway joins I-64, and is marked as the Slade or Natural Bridge exit. From this point you can use the trailhead directions to access the desired trail.

Trail Details

The trail direction was chosen by the volunteer that scouted the trail and is not a preferred or required route. If you choose to walk the trail in the opposite direction, you will need to make adjustments to the description in order to determine your bearings.

Estimated times given in the Trail Descriptions are guides for the amount of time you should allow to walk the trail ONE-WAY. On many trails, you allow for a doubling of the time needed in order to make your return trip. Of course, your pace may be faster, or slower, than that of the person who scouted.

Allowed Activities

What activities are allowed depends on the area in which you are hiking. Natural Bridge State Resort Park is the most restrictive, limiting your activities to hiking and sightseeing. No pets, camping, fires, hunting, etc. are allowed. You will also not run into off-highway vehicles (OHV's), horses or mountain bikes.

Clifty Wilderness and the Red River Geologic Area are the next most restrictive. Wilderness designation restricts machine use in the area, so you would not run across OHV's, mountain bikes, chain saws, etc. You are allowed to camp here, hunting is permitted, as are pets. Fires are allowed but may be restricted due to fire danger in dry seasons. Check with the Forest Service.

Although not a wilderness area, the Forest Service manages Red River Gorge similarly to Clifty. You may run across climbers in both Clifty Wilderness and Red River Gorge as there are some popular climbing routes.

Camping

As previously stated, camping is permitted within the Red River Gorge and Clifty Wilderness. Be sure to follow Leave No Trace procedures, and follow the Forest Service guidelines for campsites - at least 200 feet from water sources and 300 feet from developed trails and roads.

As you walk the trails in this area, you may run across a campsite that is not mentioned in the trail description. We have purposely not mentioned campsites that violate Forest Service criteria and urge you to reject these "easy" camping spots and help the forest reclaim them.

Sheltowee Trace

The Sheltowee is a 254 mile long trail through Kentucky that begins just above Morehead, KY, and ends in Pickett State Park in Tennessee. Part of that mileage runs through the Red River Gorge. Trail descriptions that encompass the Sheltowee include Sheltowee #100 (two descriptions from Frenchburg to KY 11); Whittleton Branch #216; Lakeside Trail, Balanced Rock Trail and Sand Gap Trail in Natural Bridge State Park.

The only camping allowed in Natural Bridge State Park is at Whittleton Branch Campground and Millcreek Campground at KY 11. These are fee campgrounds but include shower facilities.

Walk softly, and enjoy!

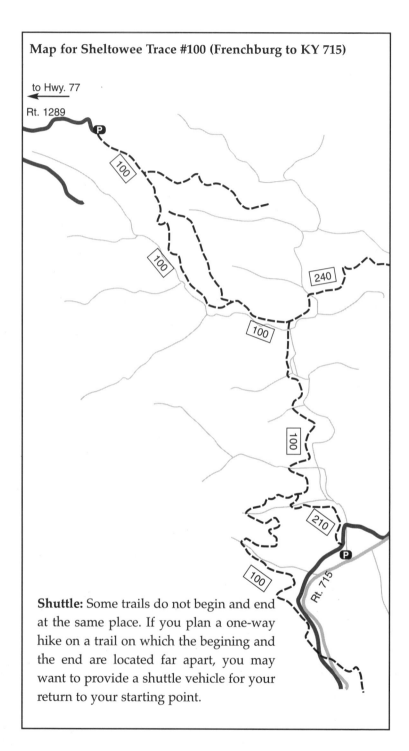

Map for Sheltowee Trace #100 (Frenchburg to KY 715)

to Hwy. 77

Rt. 1289

P

100

100

240

100

100

210

P

Rt. 715

100

Shuttle: Some trails do not begin and end at the same place. If you plan a one-way hike on a trail on which the begining and the end are located far apart, you may want to provide a shuttle vehicle for your return to your starting point.

Sheltowee Trace #100 — Frenchburg to KY 715

Shuttle Required?	Yes (See shuttle on page 32)
Length of Trail:	7.8 miles
Estimated Time:	6 1/2 hours
Difficulty:	Moderate
Net Elevation Change:	400 ft.
Highlights:	Creeks, Clifflines

Trailhead/Access: From Junior Williamson Rest Area, turn left, go under bridge to stop sign. Turn left on KY 15, go 1.5 miles to KY 77. Turn right on 77 and go 5.9 miles, passing through the Nada Tunnel, to the iron bridge. After crossing the bridge, turn right and go .8 miles to junction with KY 715. At this point go straight on 715 for 1.5 miles to Sheltowee parking lot to leave a car for the shuttle. Return to KY 77 and turn right. Go 6.5 miles, past Frenchburg Conservation Corps Camp to Corner Ridge Road. Turn Right on Corner Ridge Road and go 1 mile to trailhead parking on right.

Trail Description: Although a mostly moderate walk, part of this trail between KY 715 and Bison Way Trail (#210) have some steep climbs which are strenuous. The northern trailhead is located on the boundary of the Clifty Wilderness Area, and a portion of the trail walks through it. If you are continuing north on the Sheltowee, you will walk along the road you just drove and, later, also on KY 77.

The trail begins by following an old logging road along a ridge for the first 2 miles. It is wide and clear with good markings (diamond, diamond with turtle, Sheltowee Trace signs). Although Clifty Wilderness was designated in 1985, this road has still not reverted to any appreciable "wild" characteristics, although it is closed to motorized traffic. This is an easy and pleasant walk with a mild downhill in the last half mile. At .4 miles from the trailhead, a side trail joins from the left. This trail is on Forest Service maps but is not named and wanders out a small side ridge.

At 2 miles, the trail joins with Trail #240 which heads southeast into other areas of the Wilderness. The Sheltowee Trace turns right and heads down to Gladie Creek and shortly crosses Salt Fork which empties into Gladie at this point. The crossing here may be difficult after heavy rains. After crossing Salt Fork, watch carefully for trail signs. Sheltowee heads right and uphill from this point. The trail that follows the creek is not correct and will cause you to double back.

From this point the trail takes on more wilderness characteristics, being narrower and seemingly less used. Trail markings are more sporadic here, causing the hiker to wonder if they have strayed. Keep your eyes open for diamond blazes, although the trail path seems clear enough. During this stretch, the Sheltowee remains above Gladie Creek and traverses three drainages, Garrett, Hale & Klaber Branches. Watch for trail signs at these points, especially at Klaber Branch crossing. At this point, the Sheltowee once again goes uphill and to the right. Shortly after crossing Klaber Branch, the trail leaves the Wilderness Area and continues on Forest Service land. At 4.2 miles a trail appears on the left with a sign with no markings. This may be mistaken as Bison Way junction but is not. The Bison Way Trail (#210) joins the Sheltowee in another .1 mile (at 4.3 mile) and heads left, eventually leading to KY 715 near the Gladie Historic Site. The Sheltowee Trace continues straight.

From this point on the trail sees heavier use by day hikers who make a loop of the Sheltowee and Bison Way Trails. From this junction the trail continues through lowland forest and rhododendron into what appears to be a box canyon. Be sure to notice the high cliffs towering above as you walk the valley floor. At 4.9 miles begin a steep ascent from the valley up the ridge side to a small arch. A set of wooden steps concludes the climb. You will have about a quarter mile of ridge walk on the Sheltowee, or you might take a side trail along the ridge top to extend your time up high. At 5.4 miles, the trail heads back down, again steeply, to the valley floor. The Sheltowee now traverses several small drainages and cuts under Cloud Splitter Rock while making its way to the Red River. There are small rises and falls to the trail during this stretch which is most notable for the rock walls, cliffs and rock houses that can be found alongside the trail and in the drainage areas. These present many opportunities to rest and contemplate.

The trail crosses KY 715 at the 7.8 mile mark after a moderate drop from its hiking elevation. If you have left a car at the trail parking area, you will need to cross KY 715 and take the parking lot side trail which begins at the suspension bridge over the Red River. This will add .4 mile to your total distance.

Bison Way Trail #210

Shuttle Required?	No
Length of Trail:	.8 miles
Estimated Time:	40 minutes
Difficulty:	Easy
Net Elevation Change:	100 ft.

Trailhead/Access: From Junior Williamson Rest Area, return to Mountain Parkway heading east. Go 7.2 miles to Exit 40, Beattyville. Turn Right on KY 15 & 715, and go .7 miles. Turn right on KY 715 and go 9.6 miles to Gladie Historic Site, on left. Park here, trail begins across road.

Trail Description: From KY 715, immediately ascend the hill on the trail gaining almost all the elevation on the trail during this short stretch. Stay on trail at switchbacks to avoid the shortcuts that hasten erosion and trail damage. From this point, there are only minor elevation changes on the way to the junction with the Sheltowee Trace (#100). At about the halfway point, you will walk through a small hemlock grove with its high branches and needle covered floor. This would be a good place to stop for a quick breather. There are 2 drainages that are crossed on log footbridges in this stretch, one before and one after the hemlock grove. At .8 miles the Bison Way Trail terminates at the Sheltowee Trace. To the left it is approximately 4 miles back to KY 715; to the right, the Sheltowee continues through the Clifty Wilderness on its way to Frenchburg & beyond.

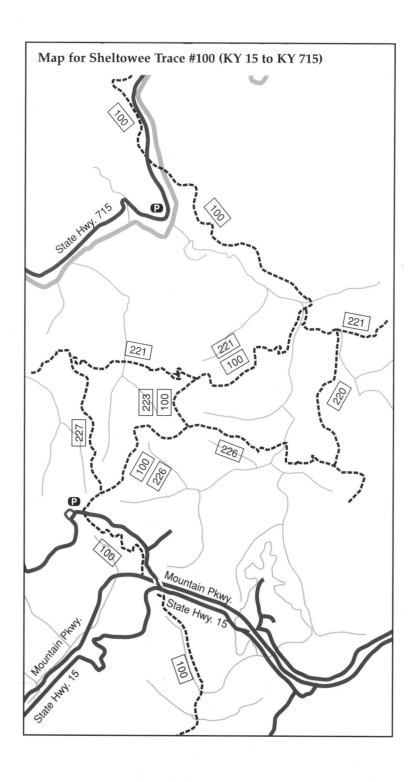

Map for Sheltowee Trace #100 (KY 15 to KY 715)

Sheltowee Trace #100 — KY 15 to KY 715

Shuttle Required?	Yes
Length of Trail:	4.7 miles
Estimated Time:	3 hours
Difficulty:	Moderate
Net Elevation Change:	500 ft.
Highlights:	Swinging Bridge, Overlooks

Trailhead/Access: From Junior Williamson Rest Area, turn left, go under bridge to stop sign. Turn right on KY 15, go 3.3 miles to Tunnel Ridge Road. Turn left on Tunnel Ridge Road. Trailhead is approximately .75 miles down Tunnel Ridge Rd. Parking area is on the left.

Trail Description: Hiking the trail from Tunnel Ridge Road is primarily downhill marked with white diamonds and a turtle. Trail markers however are not always in line of sight and some have faded. This trail has lots of rhododendron and blueberry bushes, mountain laurel and hemlocks. At the beginning of the trail there is a steep gorge to the left. Between the beginning of the trail and the junction with Rush Ridge Trail there is a beautiful wintertime view of ridge on the right. At .2 miles the trail joins with Rush Ridge Trail (#227) and Pinch-em-Tight Trail (#223). Rush Ridge Trail goes left, looping back to Gray's Arch. Continue right on the Sheltowee. From this junction the trail is primarily wide and sandy bringing you to overlooks of the Gorge before crossing a narrower ridgetop. At 1.1 miles the Sheltowee intersects with Buck Trail (#226) on the right, which leads 3 miles down to Koomer Ridge Campground. Continue left to a beautiful flat rock/ridge top that makes an ideal break spot. At 1.5 miles you reach the junction of Rough Trail (#221) and Pinch-em-Tight Tail (#223); at this junction the Sheltowee joins with Rough Trail going to the right towards the Red River. It becomes more

One of the more unique features on the Sheltowee Trace is a swinging bridge that crosses the Red River

closed-in and less used at this point. You will come across a big rock top facing south which makes a good lunch spot. After this, the trail begins losing elevation as it winds down to Chimney Top Creek, although you will encounter some uphill hiking as the trail crosses ridges. After about another .5 mile, the descent gets steeper and becomes more rocky (uneven). Soon views of Chimney Top Creek will appear as you finish your descent to make the first creek crossing. At this point you might stop to pick your way across the creek and/or have lunch or a snack. Shortly after crossing the creek, the Sheltowee and Rough Trails part, with Sheltowee continuing left towards the Red River. Shortly you will reach another creek crossing near a tree where the roots form a small dam; trail goes up the bank to the right. You have traveled approximately 3 miles to this point and will find yourself in an area of many large, old trees. The trail then crosses the creek again, this time back to the right that's a bit tricky to locate. Look for faint double mark and a 30-foot high cliff facing on the right side of the creek. There is plenty of bamboo in this area which probably floods during spring rains; be aware of weather conditions when walking this stretch. At this point the trail begins an ascent, leaving the creek and affording some views of the drainage area for Chimney Top Creek. After reaching a small ridgetop, the trail begins downhill again, using switchbacks, as it makes its approach to the Red River. At approximately 4.1 miles the trail splits, stay to the left. From here to the suspension bridge you will encounter many side trails used by hikers and fishermen. At 4.5 miles you will come to the suspension bridge that crosses the Red River. After crossing the bridge, it is .1 mile uphill to KY 715, or you can follow the trail left to the Sheltowee parking area which is .4 miles instead of the posted .1 mile.

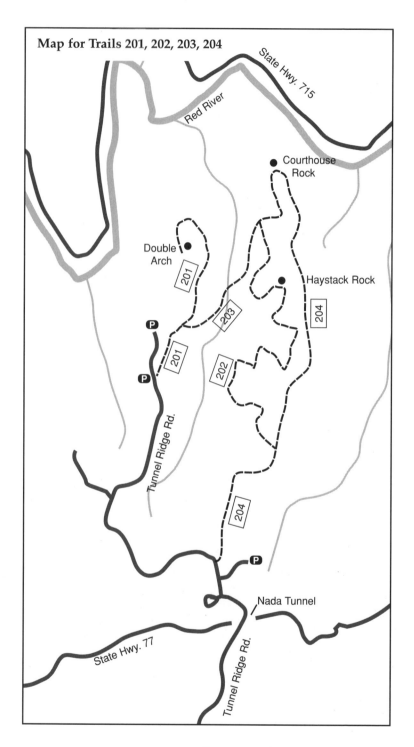

Map for Trails 201, 202, 203, 204

State Hwy. 715

Red River

Courthouse Rock

Double Arch

201

203

Haystack Rock

204

P

201

202

P

Tunnel Ridge Rd.

204

P

Nada Tunnel

State Hwy. 77

Tunnel Ridge Rd.

Double Arch Trail #201

Shuttle Required?	No
Length of Trail:	1 mile
Estimated Time:	45 minutes
Difficulty:	Easy
Net Elevation Change:	200 ft.
Highlights:	Clifflines, Arches

Trailhead/Access: From Junior Williamson Rest Area, turn left, go under bridge to stop sign. Turn right on KY 15, go 3.3 miles to Tunnel Ridge Road. Turn left on Tunnel Ridge Road. Go 4.7 miles to end of road and trailhead parking area.

Trail Description: The trail has about 40 steps at the beginning. After that the trail is fairly easy and flat. In a short distance Auxier Branch Trail (#203) connects on the right. You go straight with many lovely views of the cliffs on the left. If you are lucky you may see Double Arch here, but continue on and the trail will go around the end of the ridge until you are on the back side of the ridge. The trail climbs slightly until you find some wooden steps. Go up these to the base of Double Arch. If you are facing the arch, you should look to your right where you will find steps that will take you on top for a fine view of the valley. Return the way you came, or combine this with Auxier Branch, Auxier Ridge and Courthouse Rock Trails for a longer day at the Gorge.

Courthouse Rock Trail #202

Shuttle Required?	No
Length of Trail:	2.1 miles
Estimated Time:	1.5 hours
Difficulty:	Moderate
Net Elevation Change:	150 ft.
Highlights:	Rock formations, ridges

Trailhead/Access: From Junior Williamson Rest Area, turn left, go under bridge to stop sign. Turn right on KY 15, go 3.3 miles to Tunnel Ridge Road. Turn left on Tunnel Ridge Road. Go 3.7 miles to Auxier Ridge trailhead parking area on the right.

Trail Description: From the parking area you will experience a .75 mile hike to the junction with Auxier Ridge Trail (#204). During this distance your walk will be pretty level through a mixed hardwood forest which skirts a ravine to the right. The trail is marked with white diamond blazes with occasional views of the valley and, eventually, a nice view of Haystack Rock on the left. When you come to some small rock ledges, the trail goes to right and slightly uphill to the junction with Auxier Ridge. Take the trail left to continue on Courthouse Rock Trail (#202). At this point the trail descends very steeply through tree roots and rhododendron thickets, blocking the view in many places, then continues along the edge of a small valley, crossing many stream beds which are mostly dry. The forest canopy alternates between conifer and rhododendron with many thickets making 'tunnels' for you to walk through. At 1.5 miles there is a log seat and a side trail to a rest spot with a view of the valley. You will come to trail junction with Auxier Branch Trail (#203) at 2.5 miles. Courthouse Rock Trail continues right, uphill and sometimes steeply, along the bottom of the cliff line. The trail makes a sharp left and continues uphill through rhododendron. If you go 20 feet too far, you are under a stone outcrop or cliff. At 2.1 miles the trail joins with Auxier Ridge Trail (#204) which continues right and up, eventually climbing to Courthouse Rock on Forest Service-built steps.

Auxier Branch Trail #203

Shuttle Required?	No
Length of Trail:	.8 mile
Estimated Time:	40 minutes
Difficulty:	Moderate
Net Elevation Change:	200 ft.

Trailhead/Access: From Double Arch Trail (#201) or Courthouse Rock Trail (#202)

Trail Description: This trail connects Double Arch Trail (#201) and Courthouse Rock Trail (#202). Begin at Courthouse Rock Trail, starting downhill on minor switchbacks. As you descend, the trail becomes less rocky and could become muddy and slippery during rains as water runs down the trail. When you reach Auxier Branch you will find many 'No Camping' signs as the trail follows the stream bed with the creek on the right side. You will then cross the creek on rocks, or wade (for it is seldom very deep), then begin a short, steep uphill climb through many trees until you join with Double Arch Trail (# 201).

Auxier Ridge Trail #204

Shuttle Required?	No
Length of Trail:	2.1 mile
Estimated Time:	1 1/2 hours
Difficulty:	Easy
Net Elevation Change:	100 ft.
Highlights:	Rock formations, ridge views

Trailhead/Access: From Junior Williamson Rest Area, turn left, go under bridge to stop. Turn right on KY 15, go 3.3 miles to Tunnel Ridge Road. Turn left on Tunnel Ridge Road. Go 3.7 miles to Auxier Ridge trailhead parking area on right.

Haystack Rock

Trail Description: Auxier Ridge Trail is a 2 mile ridge walk to Courthouse Rock. Combined with the Courthouse Rock Trail it makes an excellent 5 mile loop. The trailhead can be found at the left side of the parking area and begins with a mild descent through rhododendron to a hardwood cove area. The trail at this point has mild ups and downs while crossing ridge tops. At one point, approx. .6 miles in, there is a drop in the trail. Note that to the left there is a rhododendron thicket, while to the right , a thinner growth of smaller mountain laurel is predominant. Throughout this portion, you will catch glimpses of ridge views.

At just under a mile, Auxier Ridge Trail joins with Courthouse Rock Trail (#202). Courthouse Rock Trail goes left and, 2 miles later, climbs Courthouse Rock to rejoin the Auxier Ridge Trail. Auxier Ridge Trail continues straight ahead. After leaving the trail junction the trail turns left along Auxier Ridge. Trail blazes are less common here, but the trail is well-used and obvious. Keep a lookout fo views of Ravens Rock to your right.

At about 1.75 miles, this trail becomes pretty spectacular. Much of the trail is bare rock over a narrow ridge with excellent views of the Red River Gorge in both directions. Be careful in this area because of the drop-offs. There is plenty of room for walking, but the cliffs are not fenced and common sense should be used when approaching the edge. There are plenty of opportunities here for breathtaking views, excellent pictures and relaxing stops. The trail continues like this up to Courthouse Rock where you can stop, or continue on down the Forest Service built steps to the junction with Courthouse Rock Trail (#202). You may retrace your steps to the parking area or return via trail #202 to complete the loop.

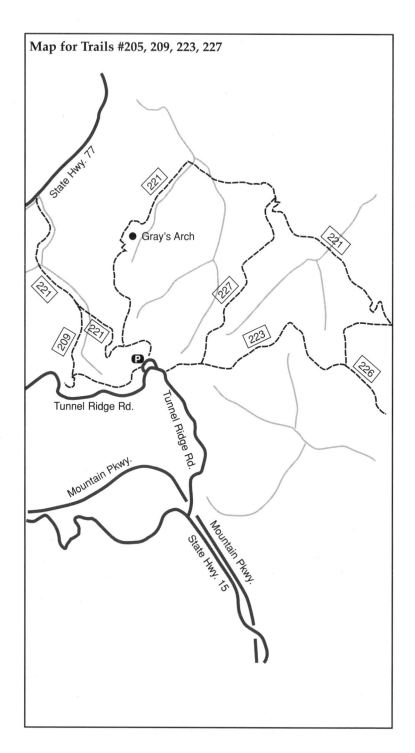

Map for Trails #205, 209, 223, 227

State Hwy. 77

221

● Gray's Arch

221

221

221

227

209

223

226

P

Tunnel Ridge Rd.

Tunnel Ridge Rd.

Mountain Pkwy.

Mountain Pkwy.

State Hwy. 15

Gray's Arch #205

Shuttle Required?	No
Length of Trail:	1.1 mile
Estimated Time:	45 minutes
Difficulty:	Easy
Net Elevation Change:	200 ft.
Highlights:	Arch, overlook

Trailhead/Access: From Junior Williamson Rest Area, turn left, go under bridge to stop sign. Turn right on KY 15, go 3.3 miles to Tunnel Ridge Road. Turn left on Tunnel Ridge Road. Go 1 mile to Gray's Arch picnic area & trailhead on right.

Trail Description: From the Gray's Arch picnic area, start on Gray's Arch Trail. In about .2 mile, this will join with Rough Trail (#221) for the rest of its distance; turn right on the combined trail. Within a quarter mile, you will pass through a meadow with opportunity for wildflower and bird identification. Be aware of several

unmarked trails in this area as the trail gradually descends on its way to Gray's Arch. At .9 mile you reach a point level with Gray's Arch that affords a beautiful overlook of the arch and the gorge below. Shortly after you will encounter a Forest Service built staircase that leads down to a junction with the side trail that leads to Gray's Arch. Take time here to rest and relax in the shadow of the arch.

View from under Gray's Arch

Return by the same trail, or follow Rough Trail (#221) to Rush Ridge (#227) and Pinch'em Tight (#223) trails to form a short loop hike.

D. Boon Hut Trail, #209

Shuttle Required?	No
Length of trail:	.6 miles
Estimated Time:	45 minutes
Difficulty:	Easy
Net Elevation Change:	None
Highlights:	Indian Petroglyphs
	Rock overhang

Trailhead/Access: From Junior Williamson Rest Area, turn left, go under bridge to stop sign. Turn right on KY 15, go 3.3 miles to

Tunnel Ridge Road. Turn left on Tunnel Ridge Road and go 1 mile to Gray's Arch Picnic Area on right; trailhead is near west entrance to picnic/parking area.

Trail Description: The trailhead is picked up at the west entrance to the Gray's Arch picnic/parking area. The trail immediately starts downward and after about 150 yards, you will descend 45 steps. At the foot of the steps there is a spur trail that goes off to the right. The actual D. Boon Hut Trail, however, goes straight ahead. You should take the trail to the right where you will come upon a large overhang. Back under the overhang a chain link fence has been erected around a large rock which does contain an Indian petroglyph. This appears in the form of a carving in the rock. After taking sufficient time to enjoy this area, retrace your steps back to the foot of the staircase and take the trail alongside the rock cliff. Very soon you will descend a set of stairs. Take time to observe the interesting rock patterns on the cliff line to your left. There will be several small streams or wet areas which ordinarily present no problem. At about .6 mile there is a fork in the trail. It is marked, but not too clearly. The D. Boon Hut Trail goes to the left up several log steps. If you continue straight, you will ultimately encounter a trail fork with Rough Trail. The large overhang immediately above the log steps is called Boone Crag. Follow the trail to the right and in about five minutes you will see the Hut area under a very large rock overhang. Once again, there is a chain link fence to protect the area. The Hut is a small shelter made of wooden shingles. It is interesting to speculate on whether D. Boone actually spent a winter in this area or not. You return by the same trail, which will take about half an hour.

Pinch 'em Tight #223

Shuttle Required?	No
Length of trail:	1.7 mile
Estimated Time:	1 1/4 hour
Difficulty:	Easy
Net Elevation Change:	none
Highlights:	Ridgetop views

Trailhead/Access: From Junior Williamson Rest Area, turn left, go under bridge to stop sign. Turn right on KY 15, go 3.3 miles to Tunnel Ridge Road. Turn left on Tunnel Ridge Road. Go .9 miles to Gray's Arch Picnic Area & Trailhead.

Trail Description: The Pinch'em Tight and Rush Ridge trails are almost completely ridgetop trails and consist primarily pine of and assorted hard woods with a lot of blueberries and mountain laurel. There are numerous overlook sites along both of these trails that give you a good impression of the nature of the Gorge area. There is no water on either of these trails.

Park at the Gray's Arch Picnic Area and begin your hike by backtracking on Tunnel Ridge Road for slightly over .1 mile to the Pinch'em Tight Trailhead on the left. Take this trail and at approximately .3 mile you will arrive at the Rush Ridge Trail (#227) junction. Rush Ridge Trail is one mile long and terminates at the Rough Trail (#221).

Continuing on the Pinch'em Tight Trail, at mile 1.2 there is a side trail to the right and down to a possible campsite. Less than .1 mile further on the trail you reach the junction with Buck Trail (#226). Go left and continue on #223 until mile 1.7 and the terminus of the Pinch'em Tight Trail. At this junction the Rough Trail (#221) descends to the left. If you turn left and follow Rough Trail for .9 mile, you will reach the junction with Rush Ridge Trail (#227), and can use this as a day loop trail.

Rush Ridge #227

Shuttle Required?	No
Length of Trail:	1.3 miles (includes part of Pinch'em Tight Trail (#223)
Estimated Time:	1 hour
Difficulty:	Easy
Net Elevation Change:	None
Highlights:	Ridgetop views

Trailhead/Access: From Junior Williamson Rest Area, turn left, go under bridge to stop sign. Turn right on KY 15, go 3.3 miles to Tunnel Ridge Road. Turn left on Tunnel Ridge Road. Go 1 mile to Gray's Arch picnic area & trailhead on right.

Trail Description: Park at the Gray's Arch picnic area and begin your hike by backtracking on Tunnel Ridge Road for slightly over .1 mile to the Pinch'em Tight Trailhead on the left. Take this trail and at approximately .3 mile you will arrive at the Rush Ridge Trail (#227) junction. Take the left on Rush Ridge, which is one mile long. This terminates at the Rough Trail (mile 1.3).

Use this trail, with Rough Trail (#221) and Gray's Arch Trail (#205) to form a short day loop.

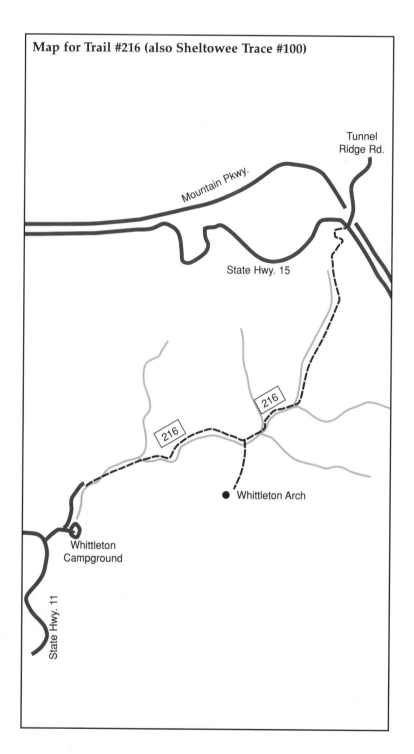

Map for Trail #216 (also Sheltowee Trace #100)

Tunnel Ridge Rd.

Mountain Pkwy.

State Hwy. 15

216

216

Whittleton Arch

Whittleton Campground

State Hwy. 11

Whittleton Branch Trail #216

Whittleton Arch Trail #217

Shuttle Required?	No, but it is an alternative
Length of Trail:	2.5 miles.
Estimated Time:	1.5 hours
Difficulty:	Easy
Net Elevation Change:	less than 1000 ft.
Highlights:	Arch

Directions to Trailhead/Access: Turn right out of the Junior Williamson Rest Area and head toward Natural Bridge State Resort Park. Pass the entrance to Hemlock Lodge on the right and take the very next left into Whittleton Branch Campground. It is approximately 2.3 miles from the rest area. There is parking on the right for hikers just past the check-in booth.

Trail Description: The Whittleton Branch Trail begins at the end of the Whittleton Branch Campground at Natural Bridge State Resort Park and ends at Hwy. 15 at the beginning of Tunnel Ridge Road. The Whittleton Arch Trail begins midway down the Whittleton Branch Trail and ends at Whittleton Arch.

A shuttle can be run if one wanted only to hike the trail one way. A nice trip can be made by leaving a car at Hemlock Lodge at Natural Bridge, shuttling to Hwy. 15, hiking the trail from there to the lodge and having lunch or dinner

The trail distances for this hike are: 0.2 miles from the parking area at Whittleton Branch Campground to the trail head, 0.8 miles from the trail head to Whittleton Arch trailhead, 0.2 miles from Whittleton Arch trailhead to the arch and 0.2 back, 1.1 miles from there to Hwy. 15.

This trail is in the bottom of a valley and follows Whittleton Branch, a perennial mountain stream. The area along the trail consists of second-growth mesophytic forest and has canopy cover which overhangs close to 100% of the trail. Dominant canopy tree species along the trail are tulip tree, sugar maple, hemlock, white pine, beech, sycamore, and white oak. Thickets under the canopy are predominantly spicebush, pawpaw, rhododendron, American hazelnut, and common alder. In the spring and summer, this is one of the best wildflower areas in the gorge. You can find yellow lady slipper, trillium, a vast array of violets, wood betony, spotted wood Lily, Jacob's ladder, bloodroot, hepatica, and many more. There is also an abundance of scouring rush along this trail.

Another interesting feature on this trail is Whittleton Arch. The Whittleton Arch Trail begins 1 mile from the trail parking area and heads off to the right. This is one of the very few arches in the Gorge that is formed by water. It is called a waterfall step arch (Silvermine is the other arch in this area that is a waterfall step arch). An arch of this type begins when a waterfall with a steep drop falls on erosion resistant sandstone. The waterfall washes away weaker sedimentary layers below, leaving a shelf. Eventually, the retreating waterfall hits a weak segment in the harder sandstone strata such as a joint fracture and undermines the shelf and isolates it, creating an arch. This arch is very hard to photograph because it's span is one of the widest in the Gorge (approximately 100 feet), and there is no way to get very far from it. This is a great lunch spot.

This trail was an old railroad bed for the Mountain Central Railroad which operated up until 1928. The tracks ran up this valley and crossed the creek about 26 times in less than two miles. There is still some evidence along the way that this was a railroad bed.

Map for Trails #206, 208, 225

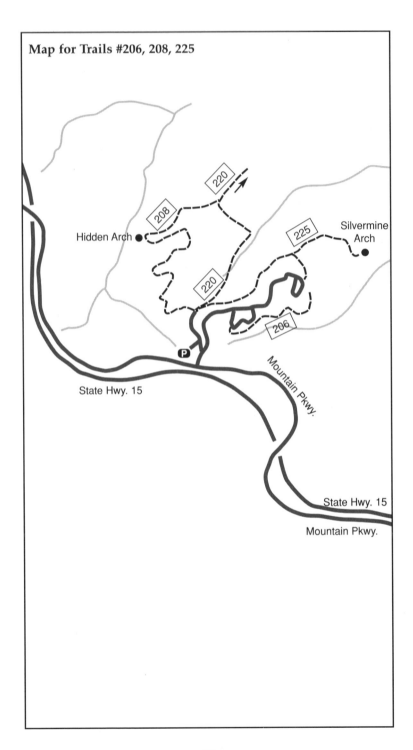

Cliff Trail #206

Shuttle Required?	No
Length of Trail:	.8 mile
Estimated Time:	45 minutes
Difficulty:	Easy
Net Elevation Change:	none
Highlights:	Ridge views

Trailhead/Access: From Junior Williamson Rest Area, turn left, go under bridge to stop sign. Turn right on KY 15, go 5.1 miles to Koomer Ridge Campground Road. Turn left into the campground and follow road .1 mile, to left, to trailhead parking area. To access the Cliff Trail, you must walk .5 mile into Koomer Ridge Campground. The trail begins across the road from campsite #13.

Trail Description: Cliff Trail is a short trail in Koomer Ridge Campground that follows the cliff line and ultimately ends near the beginning of Silvermine Arch Trail (#225) and campsite #35. For the most part there is a split rail fence marking the cliff edge and several views into the valley below. You will find yourself looking at the crowns of trees growing on the valley floor, along with several views across.

From its beginning near campsite #13, the trail drops mildly to the cliff line and bears left. There are many side trails from the campground joining this trail, but if you keep the fence to your right you will be fine. At about .1 mile, a small stone 'amphitheater' is found. If you are an early riser and are camping at Koomer Ridge, this would make a fine spot to bring a thermos of coffee and your granola bars to view the sunrise. The trail then continues along the cliff to other views and, ultimately, to its end near campsite #35.

Pay attention to the cliff and the trails when walking here. The trail is not fully developed, and user side trails may confuse you. At some points the fence may be absent, and with forest growth, the cliff edge is not readily apparent until you are upon it. From the end of the trail you may retrace your steps, walk through the campground or decide to walk Silvermine Arch Trail (#225) which begins nearby.

Hidden Arch Trail #208

Shuttle Required?	No
Length of Trail:	1 mile
Estimated Time:	45 minutes
Difficulty:	Easy
Net Elevation Change:	None
Highlights:	Arch

Lane E. Boldman photograph

View of Hidden Arch

Trailhead/Access: From Junior Williamson Rest Area, turn left, go under bridge to stop sign. Turn right on KY 15, go 5.1 miles to Koomer Ridge Campground Road. Turn left into the campground and follow road .1 mile, to left, to trailhead parking area. The trail begins across the road from the trail parking area.

Trail Description: The trailhead is just across the campground road from the trail parking area. After another 100 yards, the trail intersects with Koomer Ridge Trail (#220) and Silvermine Arch Trail (#225) which go to the right. Hidden Arch Trail goes to the left, crosses the campground roadway, passes by campsites #46 and #48, bears to the left and enters the forest. The trail is fairly level, featuring mixed hardwoods. After about 25 minutes (.75 mile) the trail takes a hard turn to the right and starts down into the rhododendron. At this point, take time to step out to a point on your left for the view. You descend 27 steps going about another 100 feet and you will encounter the rather small Hidden Arch nestled in the far corner of a small rock overhang. At this point the Hidden Arch Trail ends and the easy way is to return on the same trail you just traveled. However, you may continue to the Koomer Ridge Trail (#220) to make a loop hike.

The trail proceeds down another 35 steps with a cliff line to your right. At about 40 minutes you will reach the low point of the trail and start up 13 steps passing a spring coming in from your right. It is a fairly steep ascent. At a little over 1 mile there is a large tree across the trail and a clearing. There is a sign indicating that you should proceed straight across the clearing. The trail does descend a little at this point and a little short of 1 hour the trail should end at an intersection with the Koomer Ridge Trail (#220). Follow the Koomer Ridge Trail to your right, crossing a small draw that is solidly covered with ferns. Soon you will walk along a creek to your left that has cut a small crevice, and the creek at one point takes a precipitous drop. If there were more water, this would be an impressive waterfall. You are getting close to the campground and there will be a number of trails wandering in the area. A little over a mile and a half and probably about an hour and ten minutes, the trail forks. It is not clearly marked at this point, but the trail to the left is the official trail. If you go to the right, in about 500 feet you will return to campsite #46 and can walk out through the campground road. Proceeding to the left, however, in about 100 feet you will come to an intersection with Silver Mine Arch Trail (# 225). At this point you are retracing your original trail and in about 15 minutes should return to the trail head. The entire loop will take around an hour and a half.

Silvermine Arch Trail, # 225

Shuttle Required?	No
Length of trail:	1.4 miles
Estimated Time:	45 minutes
Difficulty:	Easy
Net Elevation Change:	None
Highlights:	Arch, ridge views

Trailhead/Access: From Junior Williamson Rest Area, turn left, go under bridge to stop sign. Turn right on KY 15, go 5.1 miles to Koomer Ridge Campground Road. Turn left into the campground and follow road .1 mile, to left, to trailhead parking area. Trailhead is across the road from the 'trail parking' area.

Trail Description: Pick up the trailhead just across from the 'trail parking' area. After about 100 yards, the trail forks - stay to the left (even though the trail marker says Trail #220). After about another 100 yards or so, Hidden Arch Trail (#208) cuts off to the left and Koomer Ridge Trail (#220) & Silvermine Arch Trail (#225) go to the right. In about 10 minutes, you will arrive at a trail crossing. Koomer Ridge Trail (#220), will go to the left while Silvermine Trail proceeds straight across. Shortly thereafter, the amphitheater will be on the right and just past the amphitheater, you will see a Forest Service road. Go straight across the road, You should see a white triangle on the far side of the road. These triangles are scattered throughout the trail. However, do not rely upon these for your directions. They are too intermittent. After about 15 minutes you will encounter a cleared area. The trail has been rerouted to the lower side of the cleared area. As the trail proceeds, the campground will be to your right. Shortly after, there will be a fork in the trail. There is a sign indicating that Silvermine Arch trail goes to the left. At this point you begin to leave the sounds of the campground. In about half an hour, or shortly over one mile, the trail

starts downward. Look for a great view to your left. BE CAREFUL however, as there is a sheer drop. Shortly thereafter, you will encounter wooden stairs and you will descend 89 steps. During this you will enter the area of rhododendron. In about 10 minutes you will descend 65 more steps. There will be a tall cliff line to your right. After you've gone approximately 1.4 miles, or around 45 minutes, you will come upon Silvermine Arch. It is a low arch nestled in the cliff line. There are some rather interesting erosion pat-

The Upper Red River running at low water

terns in the rock areas. There are a number of unofficial paths around the arch. After taking sufficient time to enjoy the area, you will start back up. First the 65 steps, then shortly thereafter the 89 steps. After this the trail is fairly level. When you get back to the crossroad near the amphitheater, you will observe a trail sign for Koomer Ridge Trail (#220) which is out of place. Continue to retrace your steps back to the beginning. The entire trip should take about 1 and one-half hours walking time.

Map for Trails #220, 226

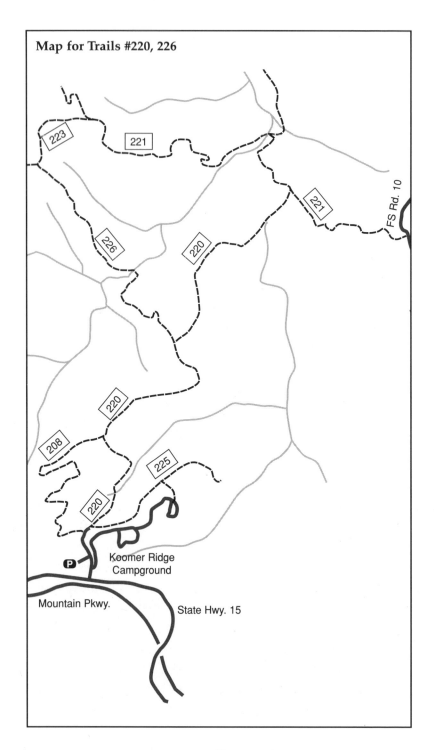

Koomer Ridge #220

Shuttle Required?	No
Length of Trail:	4.5 miles
Estimated Time:	3 3/4 hour
Difficulty:	Easy
Net Elevation Change:	420 ft.
Highlights:	Wildflowers, waterfall

Trailhead/Access: From Junior Williamson Rest Area, turn left, go under bridge to stop sign. Turn right on KY 15, go 5.1 miles to Koomer Ridge Campground Road. Turn left into the campground and follow road .1 mile, to left, to trailhead parking area. Trailhead is across the road from the trail parking area.

Trail Description: At the trailhead parking area start by going back towards the campground. Beside the campground caretaker's trailer you should see a trail sign showing Koomer Ridge Trail (#220). The trail winds its way through the campground for a few hundred yards.

As you leave the area of the campground the Koomer Ridge Trail forks and continues to the right. To the left is the Hidden Arch Trail (#208). A short bit further the trail forks again and goes left. Silvermine Arch Trail (#225) goes off to the right.

The trail continues along a nice forest corridor crossing a foot bridge or two as this section of trail can be muddy most of the year. After about a half mile, look for a waterfall formed by the creek you've been following. Shortly after, cross the creek and continue down the trail. At three quarters of a mile you reach the intersection with Hidden Arch Trail (#208). Keep right and continue on Koomer Ridge Trail. You can usually find Lady Slippers in this area during the growing season.

Around 1.25 miles there is a large, grassy, over grown area. At 1.6 miles you come to an intersection with Buck Trail (#226) which can be utilized to form a loop back to the campground. The Koomer Ridge Trail continues to the right. Look for more lady slippers and wild iris in the area.

The trail gently rolls along offering many nice views as it traverses the top of the ridge. At the end of the ridge the trail descends to the valley floor. Watch for switchbacks as you go down and stay on the trail. Look for the nice rock outcroppings and drainage crossings as you continue down to Chimney Top Creek. This area is posted 'No Camping' because of overuse, but still makes a great lunch spot. Continue on the trail and at 2.9 miles come to an intersection that marks the end of Koomer Ridge Trail.

At this point you can use Rough Trail (#221) to form numerous hikes. The most obvious is to follow Rough Trail to the Sheltowee Trace (#100) ending up on KY 715 at the Red River. Or you can use Rough Trail, with Pinch'em Tight Trail (#223) and Buck Trail (#226) to form a loop which will return you to Koomer Ridge Campground.

A view under Whittleton Arch

Buck Trail #226

Shuttle Required?	No
Length of Trail:	1.5 miles
Estimated Time:	1 1/4 hour
Difficulty:	Easy
Net Elevation Change:	400 ft.
Highlights:	Rock house, wildflowers

Trailhead/Access: The Buck Trail (#226) is a connector trail between Koomer Ridge Trail (#220) and Pinch'em Tight Trail (#223). The trail ends are accessed from either of these trails.

Trail Description: From the Pinch'em Tight Trailhead (#223), walk 1.3 miles to the junction with Buck Trail (#226), which will be to your right. The sign here shows that it is 3.0 miles to Koomer Ridge. As you continue down the trail we start to descend the ridge through a series of switchbacks. Look for a small rock house on the left before you ford the creek.

You will hike along the creek until you arrive at the confluence of two creeks. Here the trail starts back up the ridge. As you continue up the ridge look for lady slippers in March - May. At the top of the ridge you will come to the junction with Koomer Ridge Trail (#220) after 1.5 miles.

Map for Trail #207

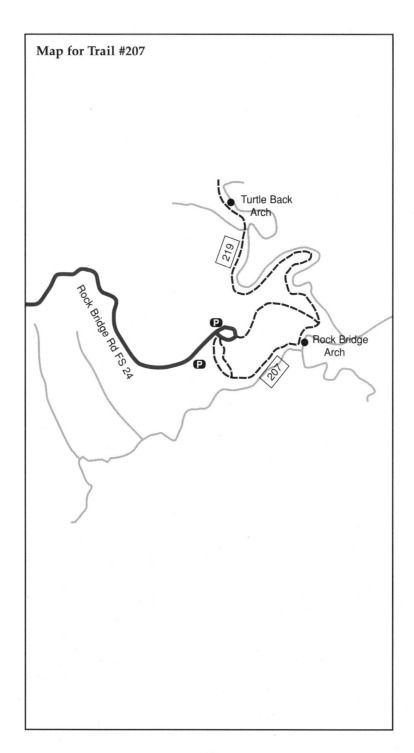

Rock Bridge #207

Shuttle Required?	No
Length of trail:	1.4 miles
Estimated Time:	1 hour
Difficulty:	Easy
Net Elevation Change:	150 ft.
Highlights:	Arch, waterfall

Trailhead/Access: From Junior Williamson Rest Area, turn left, get back on Mountain Parkway east. Go 7.2 miles to Exit 40, Beattyville. Turn Right on KY 15 & 715, and go .7 miles. Turn right on KY 715 and go .4 miles and turn right at the Rock Bridge sign. Go 3.1 miles to the Rock Bridge picnic area and parking lot. The Rock Bridge picnic area has quite a few tables and cooking areas. There are also several pit toilets. Park here and look for the trailhead sign for Rock Bridge Trail #207.

Trail Description: The trail is mostly paved and uses steps for most of the major up and down sections. This is a very easy trail and provides a nice access to the wilderness area that can be explored in more detail on the Swift Camp Creek Trail (#219). The trail is 1.4 miles long and goes through mostly hardwood and hemlock with lots of holly, rhododendron and mountain laurel.

The path begins by descending easily to the creek. The going is pretty easy and at around .6 mile you come to a small falls on the Rock Bridge fork with an overlook area. Just slightly further you come to the junction of Rock Bridge fork and Swift Camp Creek with the Rock Bridge Arch just past this confluence. There are plenty of places to relax and take a break in this area and you should take advantage of them. Continuing on, at .9 mile you come to the junction with Swift Camp Creek Trail (#219). The Rock Bridge Trail turns left and heads back up to the parking area. At just over 1 mile you come to an overlook that provides a nice view of the area. Continue on to the parking area.

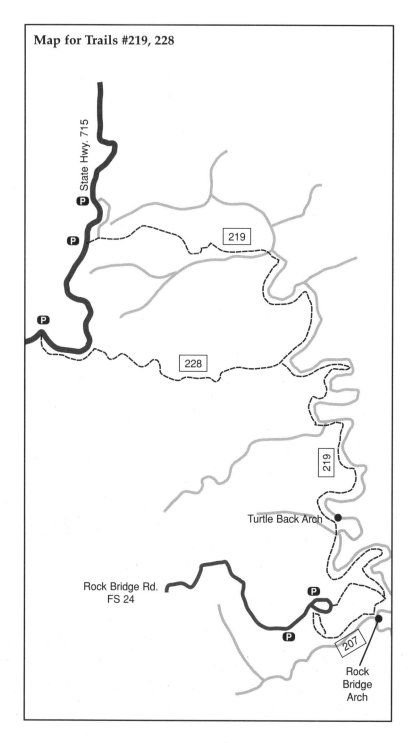

Map for Trails #219, 228

State Hwy. 715

219

228

219

Turtle Back Arch

Rock Bridge Rd.
FS 24

207

Rock
Bridge
Arch

Swift Camp Creek Trail #219

Shuttle Required?   Yes. Park at Rock Bridge Picnic Area and at either the Angel Windows Parking Area or the Swift Camp Creek/Rough Trail Parking Area.

Length of trail:	7.6 miles
Estimated Time:	4+ hours
Difficulty:	Moderate
Net Elevation Change:	250 ft.
Highlights:	Relics, waterfall, boulders

Trailhead/Access: From Junior Williamson Rest Area, return to Mountain Parkway heading east. Go 7.2 miles to Exit 40, Beattyville. Turn Right on KY 15 & 715, and go .7 miles. Turn right on KY 715 and go 4 miles to the Angel Windows Parking Area or 4.2 miles to the Swift Camp Creek/Rough Trail Parking area to drop one vehicle of the shuttle. Then backtrack on 715, about 3.5 miles, to the sign for the Rock Bridge Picnic Area. Turn left and go 3.1 miles to the picnic area and parking lot.

Trail Description: After parking at the Rock Bridge Picnic Area you will see the Rock Bridge Trailhead sign. On the opposite side of the picnic area is another marked trailhead with small signs. Take the Rock Bridge Trail (#207) down to the creek and at .5 miles you will come to the junction with the Swift Camp Creek Trail (#219) which heads off to the left. Most of this trail is along or above the creek with several cuts away from the creek only to come back to creekside fairly quickly. You will mainly be hiking through mixed hardwoods and hemlocks with some getting to be fairly large size in the interior. In addition quite a bit of the trail is canopied with rhododendron that at times can be quite thick. A hiking stick can be quite useful at times on this trail.

On Swift Creek Trail (#219) you begin on an old logging road beside the creek. At .7 miles you come to a sign for an old logging dam on the creek to your right. You will keep the creek to your right the entire trip until you head up and out. At around 1.5 miles you come to a small bridge over Bearpen Branch and then follow the stream up for a short ways until the trail turns sharply to your right. About 100 yards further on the trail you will find a side trail to the left. If you follow this side trail up, taking the left fork, you will come to an old moon shine still that is fenced off under a rock overhang. This is not very far off the main trail and is very interesting. How did they get in and out of there is the question?

Return to the main trail and continue on until you come to a creek access which you must climb down but will reward you with a small waterfall. Continuing on the main trail, you step across just above the waterfall. Staying on the main trail, you will begin a fairly steep descent with a short climb down to Reffits Branch Fork at 3.3 miles. If you follow the fork to the right about 100 yards you will come to the junction with Swift Camp Creek.

Back on the main trail watch for the blazes leading away from the fork as you wind between some very large boulders. The trail returns to the creek later and eventually you walk under a large rock overhang with water dripping on you as you come back out. At 4.5 miles you reach the junction with the Wildcat Trail (#228). Just past this junction you step over Wildcat Creek. At 5.2 miles you come up to a rocky spine where the trail makes a sharp left and follows the spine up and over; keep an eye out for the blazes through here. Just past this spine you step over a small stream and can view a dripping waterfall from a rock overhang. From here the trail takes you back down to creek level with numerous access spots. At mile 6.2 beside a large rock to your right is access to the creek. From here the trail soon turns left and begins the ascent. Be on the lookout for a very large rock overhang that is quite impressive. At 7.4 miles the trail forks with the left fork taking you to the Angel Windows Parking Area which is .1 mile away, or the right fork takes you to the Swift Camp Creek/Rough Trail Parking Area .3 mile away.

Wildcat #228

Shuttle Required?	No; unless combined with part of Swift Creek Trail
Length of trail:	1.8 miles
Estimated Time:	Less than one hour
Difficulty:	Easy
Net Elevation Change:	300 ft.

Trailhead/Access: From Junior Williamson Rest Area, return to Mountain Parkway heading east. Go 7.2 miles to Exit 40, Beattyville. Turn Right on KY 15 & 715, and go .7 miles. Turn right on KY 715 and go 2.8 miles to the Wildcat Trailhead parking lot on the left.

Trail Description: Park at the Wildcat Trailhead parking area and look for the trailhead marking across the road for the trail. The trail is pretty easy hiking and is 1.8 miles long. It provides access to the interior of the Clifty Wilderness and to Swift Camp Creek. The terminus of the trail is the junction with Swift Camp Creek Trail #219.

Cross the road (KY 715) and find the trail signs for 228. Within .1 mile the trail turns sharply left and parallels KY 715 until you come to an old logging road at .6 mile. Turn right on the logging road and follow it. Shortly thereafter, bear left, following the blazes. At just over 1 mile the trail bears left again and heads down and off of the old logging road. About 1.3 miles you enter a pretty thick rhododendron canopy and continue downhill with a drop off to your left and a fairly continuous rock face to your right. The trail ends at the junction with Swift Camp Creek Trail (#219) at mile 1.8.

Map for Trail #221

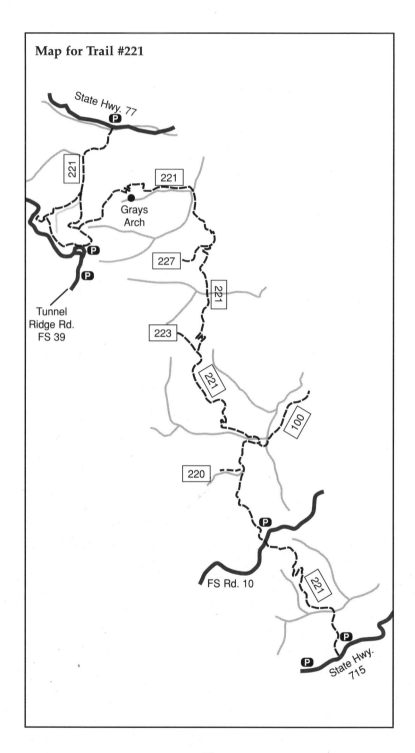

Rough Trail #221

Shuttle Required?	Yes, about 30 minute drive, one way
Length of Trail:	8.5 miles
Estimated Time:	6 hours
Difficulty:	Moderate
Net Elevation Change:	400 ft.
Highlights:	Overlooks, arches, rock houses

Trailhead/Access: Running this shuttle takes some time. From Junior Williamson Rest Area, turn left, go under bridge to stop sign. Turn left on KY 15, go 1.5 miles to KY 77. Turn right on 77 and go 3.2 miles, passing through the Nada Tunnel, to Martins Fork parking area on the left. Trail begins 100 yards southeast of parking area. Drop off hikers and gear here and begin the shuttle to Wildcat Trail Parking Area. From Martins Fork Parking area, turn left and continue 1 mile to the Iron Bridge. Turn right after the bridge on to KY 715. Continue approx. 11 miles to the Wildcat Parking Area. Leave take-out cars here and return to the Martins Fork Parking Area the way you came.

Trail Description: Rough Trail bisects the Red River Gorge from KY 77 to KY 715. As such, it is very useful in putting together loop walks within the Gorge. Besides walking its entire length, the Rough Trail provides access to Gray's Arch and Koomer Ridge, as well as joining with the Sheltowee Trace. This trail description assumes walking the entire length of the trail beginning at Martin's Fork and walking east towards Sky Bridge Road.

Once leaving KY 77, Rough Trail follows Martin's Creek for the first 3/4 mile, crossing the stream several times. Spring hikers should be aware of weather conditions and expect soggy crossings, although summer travelers will experience easier crossings. The trail is marked throughout its length with a white 221 stenciled on the trees. These blazes will at times become white diamonds marking your route.

At .3 mile a side trail goes to the right leading to Military Wall, a popular climber destination. You will find the trail fairly eroded and muddy at approximately .5 mile. Pick your way through the obstruction (remember, leave no trace) and try not to blaze new paths around the mud. For the most part, the trail remains in a valley during this stretch, traversing hemlock-beech forests and providing the naturalist with sights of ferns and other cool climate, moisture-loving plants.

At .75 mile, D. Boone Hut Trail, (#209), heads off to the right eventually ending at the Grays Arch parking lot. Rough Trail continues to the left, crossing over Martins Fork and heading uphill toward Tunnel Ridge Road. The forest begins to change at this point to oak and rhododendron. Watch for the possibility of overlooks during this stretch, with a particularly good spot at approximately 1 mile (possibility of wild blueberries if your timing is right). The trail continues up a rock grade, with stairs, until it joins Gray's Arch Trail (#205). Gray's Arch Trail goes to the right .2 mile to the parking lot. You should continue left on the combined Rough Trail-Gray's Arch Trail. Within a quarter mile, you will pass through a meadow with opportunity for wildflower and bird identification. Be aware of several unmarked trails in this area as the trail gradually descends on its way to Gray's Arch. At 2.1 miles you will encounter a Forest Service built staircase that leads down to a junction with the side trail that leads into Gray's Arch. Take time here to rest and relax in the shadow of the arch.

At the bottom of the steps Rough Trail continues to the left, continuing a gradual descent and passing rock houses, overhangs and other rock formations of interest to the hiker. At 2.5 miles it crosses King's Branch, following this stream through the valley. This part of the trail is highly used, though in good condition, and well marked. The trail begins its ascent of the next ridge at this point, reaching a set of stairs at 3 miles taking you out of the valley, with the trail reaching level ground on the ridge at approximately 3.1 miles. Blueberry thickets abound in this area as a reward to the timely traveler. At 3.2 miles, the Rush Ridge Trail (#227), joins from the right, coming up 1 mile from the Gray's Arch road. The sign here says you have come 4 miles, but is a bit premature.

At this point the trail begins a difficult descent over rocks and roots that will have you carefully picking your way. The reward is an enormous rock house at 3.3 miles which would make a good spot to relax and explore. When continuing your hike at this point, do so with care. The rock house area is filled with many side trails that look legitimate, only to end abruptly, and the trails here remain damp so watch your footing. The actual trail descends along the bottom of the rock ledges into a stream bed below the rock house. Watch for the blazes, marked on the rocks as well as trees, and you will successfully navigate this area. The trail continues its descent, becoming more narrow, then drops steeply to cross Bush Branch at 3.7 miles.

From here the trail ascends Rush to join the Sheltowee Trace (#100). On your ascent be on the lookout for an overlook of this mini-gorge (4.1 mile) and a rock house (4.2 mile). Rough Trail joins with the Sheltowee Trace and Pinch'em Tight Trail (#223) which is well marked. Pinch'em Tight Trail heads to the right 1.6 miles to the Gray's Arch Road. Rough Trail joins with the Sheltowee Trace continuing left. Look for double blazing in this stretch, the white diamond of Rough Trail and the "turtle" blaze of the Sheltowee.

A large, bare rock area will be passed at 4.5 miles. If you chance to camp near here, or are walking in the evening, this may present a good spot for stargazing. At 5 miles the trail begins a downhill grade, gradually leveling off, then descending to a spring run-off rock bed. At the bottom of this descent, you will be paralleling the Right Fork of Chimney Top Creek. Hawks are a common sight in the sky in this stretch, and springtime should bring a multitude of songbirds to this riparian area.

Rough Trail crosses the Right Fork of Chimney Top Creek at 5.5 miles, and shortly after, at 5.6 miles the Sheltowee Trace splits off left, towards the Red River. Continue straight ahead along the main branch of Chimney Top Creek to the junction with the Koomer Ridge Trail (#220) at 5.9 miles. The Koomer Ridge Trail bears right, heading to the campground 2.6 miles away. Rough Trail crosses Chimney Top Creek at this point, and is highly eroded at the creek bank. The trail ascends for the next .5 mile, passing a rock house with a potential water source and reaches the Rough Trail Parking Area at 6.5 miles. A short walk through the woods past this point will bring you to Chimney Top Road. This could be used as an alternate trailhead to this hike, cutting approximately 2 miles off the total distance.

From Chimney Top Road, the trail begins a descent into the valley, passing numerous rock houses of varying sizes and reaching Parched Corn Creek at 7.7 miles. The trail at this point is somewhat difficult because of the grade (and because you have already hiked 7 miles!). At 7.9 miles, the trail crosses Parched Corn Creek and begins its ascent to Sky Bridge Road. Along the way you will pass more rock houses and boulder formations. At 8.5 miles, Rough Trail ends at Sky Bridge Road. The Angel Windows Parking Area is to your right about .1 mile, while the Rough Trail/Swift Creek Parking Area is left about .1 mile.

Shorter Trails

Tower Rock #229

Shuttle Required?	No
Length of Trail:	.75 miles
Estimated Time:	30 minutes
Difficulty:	Moderate
Net Elevation Change:	Less than 300 ft.

Trailhead/Access: From Junior Williamson Rest Area, return to Mountain Parkway heading east. Go 7.2 miles to Exit 40, Beattyville. Turn Right on KY 15 & 715, and go .7 miles. Turn right on KY 715 and go 8.7 miles to Tower Rock Trail. Parking is on left of road across from trailhead. Note that this drive will take you down into the Gorge valley.

Trail Description: This trail is narrow but in good condition. It maintains a gradual but consistent uphill grade. At .3 miles the trail splits into a loop that goes around both sides of Tower Rock. At .4 miles the trail reaches Tower Rock. This is a large rock formation several stories high. There is access onto this structure for a view over the forest canopy.

Sky Bridge #214

Shuttle Required?	No
Length of Trail:	.17 miles
Estimated Time:	30 minutes
Difficulty:	Easy
Net Elevation Gain/Loss:	None

Trailhead/Access: From Junior Williamson Rest Area, return to Mountain Parkway heading east. Go 7.2 miles to Exit 40, Beattyville. Turn Right on KY 15 & 715, and go .7 miles. Turn right on KY 715 and

SkyBridge

go 4.9 miles to Sky Bridge Recreation Area road. It is another .3 mile to the Sky Bridge parking area and trailhead. Rest room facilities are available.

Trail Description: This is a very easy trail being mostly paved. The trail to Sky Bridge itself is only .17 miles, but a longer loop of .8 miles is available. The view from the top of this arch is quite spectacular. After crossing over the bridge follow the trail back to the parking area. There are several sets of stairs which add a little challenge to this otherwise simple hike

Angel Windows #218

Shuttle Required?	No
Length of Trail:	.3 miles
Estimated Time:	20 minutes
Difficulty:	Easy
Net Elevation Change:	None

Trailhead/Access: From Junior Williamson Rest Area, return to Mountain Parkway heading east. Go 7.2 miles to Exit 40, Beattyville. Turn Right on KY 15 & 715, and go .7 miles. Turn right on KY 715 and go 4.0 miles to Angel Windows parking area.

Trail Description: This is a good short hike for those who want to experience the Red River Gorge without a strenuous journey. The trail circles the rim of a small gorge and follows along below several rock houses and ledges. At the end of the trail (.3 miles) the hiker will find "angel windows" a double arch carved through the rock by wind. Angel Windows opens to an amphitheater of rock houses which look down into this small gorge.

Princess Arch Trail #233

Shuttle Required?	No
Length of Trail:	.4 mile
Estimated Time:	20 minutes
Difficulty:	Easy
Net Elevation Change:	50 ft.

Trailhead/Access: From Junior Williamson Rest Area, return to Mountain Parkway heading east. Go 7.2 miles to Exit 40, Beattyville. Turn Right on KY 15 & 715, and go .7 miles. Turn right on KY 715 and go 2.2 mile to Chimney Rock Road. Veer left onto Chimney Rock Road (gravel road) and go 3.6 miles to parking loop at end. Princess Arch Trailhead is immediately to the right as the road loop begins.

Trail Description: Princess Arch Trail follows a short ridgetop from the road to the Arch and proceeds to an overlook. For the most part, this trail is level and should provide little difficulty for any walker.

From the road, follow the trail, which is highly used, into the forest. You will pass maple and beech with pines, and some rhododendron thickets along the way. There are several user-made side trails, but the main branch should be easy to follow. At .1 mile, there is a small side trail that leads down and to the left. However, the main trail rounds the point and heads to the right. Shortly after this, another side trail leads to the left, which will take you down and under the arch. At .25 mile, the trail narrows and becomes a rock path over Princess Arch. To the right is a steep drop-off into the forest; to the left is a diamond blaze and a small trail. This trail snakes down the side and also provides access to the underside of the arch.

As you cross the arch, the steep drops provide fine views of the Gorge. From here, the trail ascends slightly and takes you to a fine overlook at .3 miles. There is another overlook a little further on, but there is not a maintained trail to it. You will need to scramble down the rock to access the trail to it. Watch your footing as leaves and roots make the way potentially hazardous. If you choose to reach this overlook, you will be rewarded with fine views of the Gorge, Chimney Top Rock and Cloud Splitter Rock.

When you have enjoyed the views, return the same way that you came.

Whistling Arch #234

Shuttle Required?	No
Length of Trail:	.4 miles
Estimated Time:	20 minutes
Difficulty:	Easy
Net Elevation Change:	None

Trailhead/Access: From Junior Williamson Rest Area, return to Mountain Parkway heading east. Go 7.2 miles to Exit 40, Beattyville. Turn Right on KY 15 & 715, and go .7 miles. Turn right on KY 715 and go 4.7 miles to the Whistling Arch Trail Parking Area.

Trail Description: This trail is very short and has very little elevation gain or loss. At .14 miles the trail splits - stay to the left. At .2 miles the trail comes to Whistling Arch. This is one of the beautiful arches the Red River Gorge is noted for — a good spot to explore.

Chimney Top Trail #235

Shuttle Required?	No
Length of Trail:	.25 mile
Estimated Time:	20 minutes
Difficulty:	Easy
Net Elevation Change:	None

Trailhead/Access: From Junior Williamson Rest Area, return to Mountain Parkway heading east. Go 7.2 miles to Exit 40, Beattyville. Turn Right on KY 15 & 715, and go .7 miles. Turn right on KY 715 and go 2.2 mile to Chimney Rock Road. Veer left onto Chimney Rock Road (gravel road) and go 3.6 miles to parking loop at end. Chimney Top Trailhead is at the top of the road loop.

Trail Description: Chimney Top Rock Trail begins near the top of the loop at the end of Chimney Rock Road. It is a short, mostly paved walk to an overlook that has rock and post walls to keep walkers from falling. The overlook provides fine views of the Red River Gorge valley, Cloud Splitter Rock, Half Moon Rock and Pinch'em Tight Gap. The trail itself is very wide and well used, with several side trails to overlooks of different parts of the valley. Take care when leaving the main trail, watch your footing and stay clear of ledges. Both this and Princess Arch trail have been the scene of several fatal accidents over the years. If you remain on the main trail, however, you should find your walk safe and enjoyable.

Return to the parking lot on the same trail you walked in.

Original Trail,
Natural Bridge State Resort Park

Shuttle Required?	No
Length of trail:	.5 mile
Estimated Time:	45 minutes
Difficulty:	Moderate
Net Elevation Change:	250 ft.

Trailhead access: From Junior Williamson Rest Area, turn right, go 2.2 miles to Natural Bridge State Resort Park entrance. Turn right into park, then left up to Hemlock Lodge Parking lot. Take the

Trails from Natural Bridge State Park

walkway behind the Lodge which leads to the Activity Center. Original Trail is clearly marked.

Trail Description: Original Trail is perhaps the most active trail at Natural Bridge State Park, since it leads most directly to the Natural Bridge, for which the park is named. The trail is very well maintained and clearly marked. The park service has provided several benches and one shelter along the trail, to take a break and enjoy the scenery. Although the trail is very well maintained, it is somewhat difficult due to it's rapid gain in elevation.

The view from the top of Natural Bridge is quite breathtaking, which easily explains its popularity. The hike doesn't take very long and has become a great pastime for many families. From the top of the bridge, Lookout Point can be seen directly across this gorge.

Trail Map for Natural Bridge

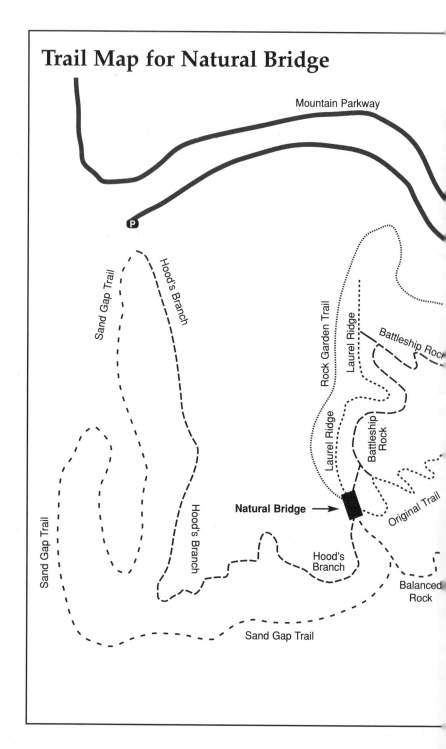

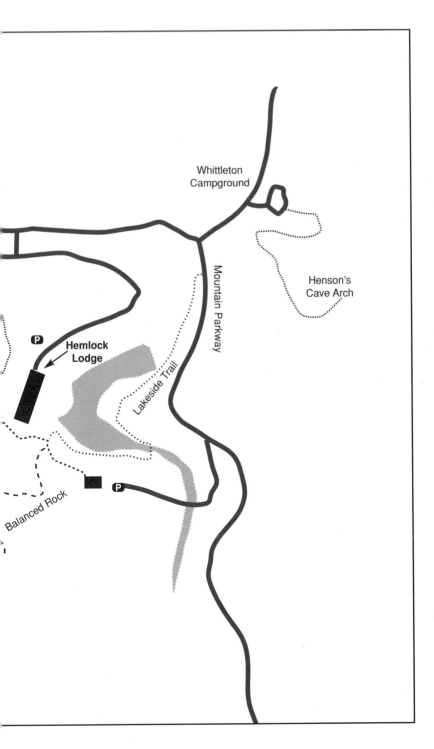

Whittleton
Campground

Henson's
Cave Arch

Mountain Parkway

P

**Hemlock
Lodge**

Lakeside Trail

P

Balanced Rock

85

Balanced Rock Trail, Natural Bridge State Resort Park

Shuttle Required?	No
Length of trail:	.75 mile
Estimated Time:	1 1/2 hours
Difficulty:	Moderate
Net Elevation Gain/Loss:	250 ft.

Trailhead access: From Junior Williamson Rest Area, turn right, go 2.2 miles to Natural Bridge State Resort Park entrance. Turn right into park, then left up to Hemlock Lodge Parking lot. Take the walkway behind the Lodge which leads to the Activity Center. Balanced Rock Trail is clearly marked.

Trail Description: Balanced Rock Trail, together with Lakeside Trail and Sand Gap Arch Trail, is part of the Sheltowee Trace through Natural Bridge State Resort Park.

After an initial set of steps, the trail turns in front of a cave entrance. If you have a flashlight, a short cave side trip is fun. Bats can usually be seen by shining your light up cracks in the ceiling. After 100 feet you will enter a large room. Turn off your flashlight at this point to look for daylight from the small exit to your right. Crawl out of this exit and turn to your right on the trail. After a short distance look for a connector trail to the right and take it back to the Balanced Rock Trail by the cave entrance.

Continue on the trail up a set of steps to Balanced Rock on your left. Immediately after the rock, 300 steps lead to the top of Natural Bridge. Be careful to bear to the right on this trail and not get on the Sand Gap Arch Trail that forks to the left just before the bridge.

Battleship Rock Trail, Natural Bridge State Resort Park

Shuttle Required?	No
Length of trail:	.75 mile
Estimated Time:	1 1/2 hours
Difficulty:	Easy
Net Elevation Change:	250 ft.

Trailhead access: From Junior Williamson Rest Area, turn right, go 2.2 miles to Natural Bridge State Resort Park entrance. Turn right into park, then left up to Hemlock Lodge Parking lot. Take the walkway behind the Lodge which leads to the Activity Center. Begin by taking the Original Trail off this walkway. Battleship Rock Trail begins to your right at the top of the first set of steps.

Trail Description: From the Original Trail, follow Battleship Rock Trail along the ridge above Hemlock Lodge until it joins with Rock Garden Trail. At this point , turn left toward Natural Bridge. At about .4 mile, the trail reaches the bottom of Devil's Gulch where you can choose to take one of two stairways - Devil's Gulch or Needle's Eye - to Laurel Ridge Trail above. Both of these routes are long wooden staircases and make an excellent side loop trail that includes views from the ridge top. However, Battleship Rock Trail takes a sharp left at this point, ascending through mixed vegetation and providing views of several rock houses until its end at the base of Natural Bridge.

Rock Garden Trail, Natural Bridge State Resort Park

Shuttle Required?	No
Length of trail:	1.75 mile
Estimated Time:	1 1/4 hrs.
Difficulty:	Moderate
Net Elevation Change:	250 ft.

Trailhead access: From Junior Williamson Rest Area, turn right, go 2.2 miles to Natural Bridge State Resort Park entrance. Turn right into park, then left up to Hemlock Lodge Parking lot. Take the walkway behind the Lodge which leads to the Activity Center. Begin by taking the Original Trail off this walkway. Rock Garden trailhead is located near the beginning of the Original Trail, off of the Battleship Rock Trail.

Trail Description: As you climb the stairs up the Original trail you notice the forest starting to suround you. At the top of the stairs the trail forks continue to the right. Battle Ship Rock Trail will be to the right as you continue down the main trail. Take it to get to the start of the Rock Garden Trail. In a few minutes you'll be skirting a cliff on your left. Notice the large boulder on the right as you cross your first bridge. Fifteen minutes along the trail you can admire all of the large rocks in this area which give the trail its name. When

you cross the second bridge look at the large projection overhead. At thirty minutes down the trail you turn away from the valley and start your climb to the top. Be carefull on the stone cut stairs which can be slippery when wet. Once you make it to the top take a break sit down and admire the view. The trail starts to wind along the cliff face giving you great views along the way. At around forty minutes the trail appears to fork again. Stay left following the cliff face. The skylift will come in to view at around fifty-five minutes on the trail. The trail will come close to the cliff face giving you a chance to see interesting patterens in the face of the rock. You round the last corner at about an hour and five minutes and will get the first view of Natural Bridge. There are several ways to return to the lodge. Take a look at the map and decide on which trail to return.

Sand Gap Arch Trail, Natural Bridge State Resort Park

Shuttle Required?	No
Length of trail:	8.5 miles
Estimated Time:	5 hours
Difficulty:	Strenuous
Net Elevation Change:	500 ft.

Trailhead access: Sand Gap trailhead is located near Natural Bridge, at the top of the Balanced Rock Trail.

Trail Description: The trail starts near Natural Bridge and can be reached by the Balanced Rock Trail, Historic Trail, or Rock Garden Trail. From the bridge itself, walk past the picnic shelter to the point where Balanced Rock Trail intersects the beginning of the Sand Gap Arch Trail. After you walk along the trail for about 10 minutes, look to the ridge to your right for an old shelter, probably constructed by the Civilian Conservation Corps. After about 40 minutes, the trail reaches a juncture. The Sand Gap Trail takes a sharp turn to the right. (The Sheltowee Trace is the trail at the juncture that continues straight ahead by going through a metal gate and across the top of White's Branch Arch.) In about a half hour you will walk past an impressive cliff line to the right of the trail and shortly thereafter, the cliffline switches to the left and there is an interesting rock house with a rounded shape. This portion of the trail is on a fairly wide old logging road. At about three and a half miles, the trail begins to descend through some area that can be quite wet in rainy weather. At about the two-hour mark, you should cross Lower Hood's Branch, then continue with the cliff line to your right. After walking a bit over three hours, you should come to another wooden bridge across Lower Hood's Branch. Next to the bridge is a small wooden bench near the edge of the stream. After crossing this bridge, take a hard right and ascend using another old logging road going about 300 yeards. The trail goes sharply to the left and can be a bit difficult to locate. The trail then goes around the edge of the hills, over some rocky area which can cause a little problem with footing, particularly in the fall when the leaves have just come down. After about four and a half hours, you should pass the end of Hood's Branch Trail, at which time you take a left down the roadway, descending rather steeply at the end to a chair lift and some maintenance buildings. From this point it is about a 20 minute walk up the main park road to the Lodge.

Hood's Branch Trail, Natural Bridge State Resort Park

Shuttle Required?	No
Length of trail:	3.8 miles
Estimated Time:	2 - 2 1/2 hours
Difficulty:	Moderate
Net Elevation Change:	400 ft.

Trailhead access: From Junior Williamson Rest Area, turn right, go 2.2 miles to Natural Bridge State Resort Park entrance. Turn right into park, then right to Skylift Parking Area. Trail begins behind Shelter #2 & miniature golf course.

Trail Description: The trail generally follows Upper Hood's Branch. It is quite steep at first. At .1 mile, the grade decreases becoming relatively flat and joining with Sand Gap Arch Trail which begins on the right. At .35 mile, a large limestone rock with a cave-like opening can be seen about 50 foot off the trail to the right. At .6 miles you pass a log shelter on the right which was built by the Civilian Conservation Corps in the 1930's.

You cross the first of several plank bridges at .8 miles, this one over a small feeder stream to Upper Hood's Branch. A word of caution: bridges and plank walkways can be slippery - tread carefully. This is quickly followed by a second bridge, then crosses a swampy area on a boardwalk. At 1 mile, you will pass through a hemlock grove.

The Trail soon climbs uphill where it passes a magnolia grove at 1.1 miles. It continues on, passing through an extensive rhododendron thicket at 1.4 miles. Mountain Laurel can be seen just before the 1.5 mile point. At this point there is a junction in the trail. Rueben's Cutoff goes straight ahead, reaching Natural Bridge in 1.5 miles. Hood's Branch Trail continues to the right, rather steeply uphill, taking a second route to Natural Bridge (2.5 miles).

The trail sweeps to the left. A rock house is seen on the right after passing striated sandstone at 1.6 miles. This is a rather deep shelter, somewhat cave-like. It has a protective log fence in front - a good rest stop. Another small rock house is encountered at 1.75 miles. This one is impressive with a large opening on the left side.

At 2 miles you will see what may be the largest and most impressive rock house in the park, perhaps as long as a football field. You cross a small bridge into it near the right end. The trail continues on through much of it. Be careful as the trail can be slippery and there is a significant drop-off on the left after you leave the bridge.

At 2.4 miles you reach a junction in the trail. Straight ahead the trail goes to the Rueben's Cutoff parking area (1.5 miles). Approaching 2.75 miles you are aware that the forest is more open with rhododendron and hemlock having given way to poplar and oak.

At 3.5 miles you cross a bridge just below yet another rock house. The trail makes a switchback uphill. The trail soon ends at Natural Bridge, having come 3.8 miles from the parking area. Ahead is Fat Man's Misery.

From this point you have several options. The shortest is the Original Trail. It is .75 miles from Natural Bridge to Hemlock Lodge parking area.

Henson's Arch Trail, Natural Bridge State Resort Park

Shuttle Required?	No
Length of trail:	.3 mile
Estimated Time:	1/2 hour
Difficulty:	Easy
Net Elevation Change:	Less than 100 ft.

Trailhead access: From Junior Williamson Rest Area, turn right, go 2.2 miles to Whittleton Branch Campground entrance. Turn left into campground and park. Walk along the campground road, towards the rest rooms. Henson's Gap Trail begins behind campsite A7.

Trail Description: Behind campsite start trail by crossing small footbridge and ascending hillside. Nearly all the elevation gain on the trail is achieved during this portion of the walk, approximately .1 mile. The trail then levels out and winds back toward the road through maple and hemlock trees. It then curves left, leaving the road and begins a gentle ascent toward a small cliff formation. It passes this cliff on the left walking up a shallow valley. Watch your footing during this stretch. The trail ends at a guard rail with steps into a double grotto connected by Henson's Arch. This is a great short trail to take to get away for awhile and relax or meditate.

Lakeside Trail, Natural Bridge State Resort Park

Shuttle Required?	No
Length of trail:	.5 mile
Estimated Time:	15 minutes
Difficulty:	Easy
Net Elevation Change:	None

Trailhead access: From Junior Williamson Rest Area, turn right, go 2.2 miles to Natural Bridge State Resort Park entrance. Turn right into park, then left up to Hemlock Lodge parking lot. Take the walkway behind the Lodge which leads to the Activity Center. At the point where Balanced Rock and Original Trail join, turn left toward snack shop for Hoe-down Island. Lakeside trail begins on footbridge over Middle Fork of Red River.

Trail Description: This is a short paved trail along the lake below Hemlock Lodge providing easy walking for all. It begins at the footbridge by Hoe-down Island and ends at a parking area on KY 11 approximately 100 yards from the Whittleton Branch Campground entrance. Lakeside trail provides a connector between Whittleton Branch Campground and Natural Bridge State Park, as well as serving as a portion of the Sheltowee Trace between Whittleton Branch Trail and Balanced Rock Trail.

Laurel Ridge Trail, Natural Bridge State Resort Park

Shuttle Required?	No
Length of trail:	.75 mile
Estimated Time:	1/2 hour
Difficulty:	Easy
Net Elevation Change:	None

Trailhead access: From Junior Williamson Rest Area, turn right, go 2.2 miles to Natural Bridge State Resort Park entrance. Turn right into park, then left up to Hemlock Lodge Parking lot. Take the walkway behind the Lodge which leads to the Activity Center. Original Trail is clearly marked.

Trail Description: Laurel Ridge Trail is easily hiked and very well maintained. The trailhead begins at one end of Natural Bridge and ends at Lover's Leap. The trail itself is relatively flat since it follows a ridge top. It is accessible from Original Trail and Balanced Rock Trail.

From Natural Bridge, Laurel Ridge Trail follows the ridge top to a beautiful rest spot, Lookout Point. From here you can look back across this gorge to see Natural Bridge, from which you have just come. From Lookout Point, continue following the ridge towards Lover's Leap, another 10-minute hike. Along the way you will pass two sets of stairs that lead down from the ridge -Devil's Gulch and Needle's Eye stairways. Both of these passages will take you to Battleship Rock Trail, which will lead you back to Original Trail. Lover's Leap provides another beautiful view of this area.

Contacts &
Phone Numbers

Daniel Boone National Forest

Headquarters, Winchester, KY (606) 745-3100
information on forest conditions, regulations, trails outside
the Red River Gorge; Sheltowee Trace

Stanton Ranger District,

Stanton, KY (606) 663-2852
information regarding Red River Gorge, Clifty Wilderness,
Koomer Ridge Campground; hours- 8:00am-4:30pm

Natural Bridge State Resort Park

(606) 663-2214
Trail conditions at Natural Bridge; lodge reservations;
camping information for Whittleton Campground and
Mill Creek Lake Campground

Police

Kentucky State Police, Morehead Post (606) 784-4127
Powell County Dispatch (606) 663-4116
Wolfe County Dispatch (606) 668-6757
Menifee Sheriff, Frenchburg, KY (606) 768-3875

Ambulance

Powell County, Well Funeral Home (606) 663-2203
Powell County, Hearne Funeral Home (606) 663-4375
Wolfe County (606) 668-3405
Menifee County (606) 768-2745

Hospital

Campton (606) 668-3120
Clark Regional Hospital (606) 745-3500

Bird Checklist

___ Ruffed Grouse

___ Yellow-billed Cuckoo

___ Red-tailed Hawk

___ Barred Owl

___ Ruby-throated Hummingbird

___ Pileated Woodpecker

___ Red-bellied Woodpecker

___ Hairy Woodpecker

___ Downey Woodpecker

___ Acadian Flycatcher

___ Eastern Phoebe

___ Eastern Wood Pewee

___ Carolina Chickadee

___ Tufted Titmouse

___ White-breasted Nuthatch

___ Carolina Wren

___ Blue-gray Gnatcatcher

___ Wood Thrush

___ Gray Catbird

___ Red-eyed Vireo

___ White-eyed Vireo

___ Yellow-throated Vireo

___ Scarlet Tanager

___ Indigo Bunting

___ Rufous-sided Towhee

___ American Goldfinch

___ Yellow-breasted Chat

Warbler Checklist

__ Blue-winged Warbler

__ Northern Parula

__ Kentucky Warbler

__ Yellow Warbler

__ Black-throated Green Warbler

__ Cerulean Warbler

__ Black and white Warbler

__ American Redstart

__ Worm-eating Warbler

__ Swainsonís Warbler

__ Ovenbird

__ Louisiana Waterthrush

__ Common Yellowthroat

__ Hooded Warbler

__ Prairie Warbler

__ Pine Warbler

__ Yellow-throated Warbler

__ Prothonotary Warbler

__ Tennessee Warbler

__ Nashville Warbler

__ Magnolia Warbler

__ Black-throated Blue warbler

__ Blackburnian Warbler

Wildflower Checklist

__ Bellwort (Uvularia perfoliata)

__ Yellow Trout-Lily (Erythronium americanum)

__ Speckled Wood-Lily (Clintonia umbellulata)

__ Solomon's-Seal (Polygonatum biflorum)

__ Crested Dwarf Iris (Iris cristata)

__ Early Spiderwort (Tradescantia virginiana)

__ Yellow Lady's-Slipper
(Cypripedium calceolus var.pubescens)

__ Pink Lady's-Slipper (Cypripedium acaule)

__ Showy Orchis (Orchis spectabilis)

__ Jack-In-The-Pulpit (Arisaema atrorubens)

__ Trillium (ssp.)

__ Wood Poppy (Stylophorum diphyllum)

__ Hairy Buttercup (Ranunculus hispidus)

__ Star Chickweed (Stellaria pubera)

__ Hepatica (Hepatica acutiloba)

__ False Rue Anemone (Isopyrum biternatum)

__ Rue Anemone (Thalictrum thalictroides)

__ May-Apple (Podophyllum pelatum)

__ Twinleaf (Jeffersonia diphylla)

__ Bloodroot (Sanguinaria canadensis)

__ Cut-leaf Toothwort (Dentaria laciniata)

__ Pennywort (Obolaria virginica)

__ Columbine (Aquilegia canadensis)

__ Red Catchfly (Silene virginica)

__ Wild Geranium (Geranium maculatum)

__ Phlox (ssp.)

__ Jacob's-Ladder (Polemonium reptans)

__ Purple Phacelia (Phacelia bipinnatifida)

__ Bluets (Houstonia caerulea)

__ Golden Ragwort (Senecio aureus)

__ Hepatica (Hepatica acutiloba)

__ Spring-beauty (Claytonia virginica)

__ Trailing Arbutus (Epigaea repens)

__ Miami Mist (Phacelia purshii)

__ Foamflower (Tiarella cordifolia)

__ Bishop's Cap (Mitella diphylla)

__ Harbinger-of-Spring (Erigenia bulbosa)

__ Stonecrop (Sedum ternatum)

__ Wood Vetch (Vicia caroliniana)

__ Wood-Betony (Pedicularis canadensis)

__ Synandra (Synandra hispidula)

__ Meehania (Meehania cordata)

__ Lyre-Leaved Sage (Salvia lyrata)

__ Dutchman's-Breeches (Dicentra cucullaria)

__ Squirrel-Corn (Dicentra canadensis)

__ Violet's (ssp.)

__ Dwarf Larkspur (Delphinium tricorne)

__ Pussy-Toes (Antennaria solitaria)

__ Dwarf Dandelion (Krigia biflora)

__ Wild Ginger (Asarum canadense)

Area Maps

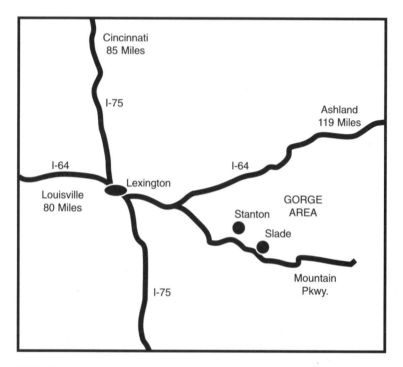

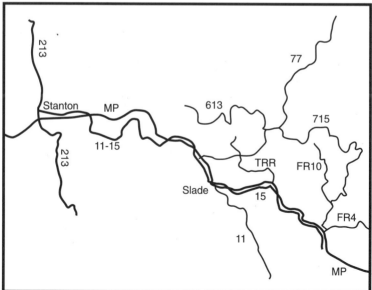

Area Maps—Gorge Trails

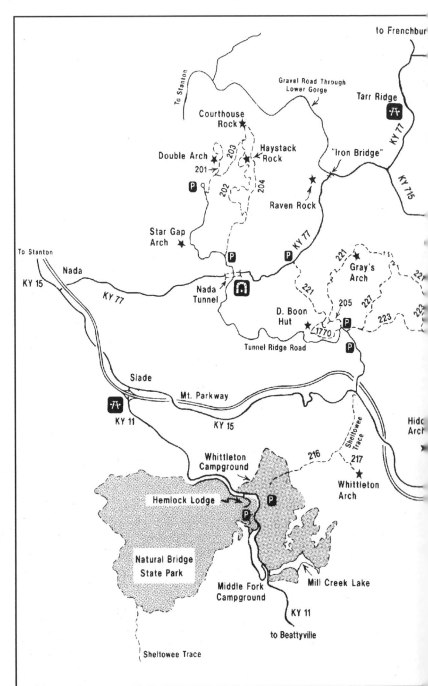

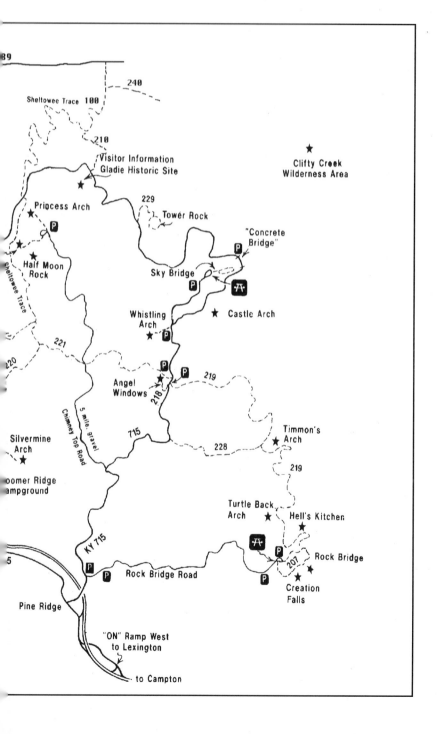